The Power of Grace

Books and Audio by David Richo

How to Be an Adult in Love: Letting Love in Safely and Showing It Recklessly
(Shambhala Publications, 2013)

Embracing the Shadow: Discovering the Hidden Riches in Our Relationships
(Shambhala Audio, 2013)

Coming Home to Who You Are: Discovering Your Natural Capacity for Love,
Integrity, and Compassion (Shambhala Publications, 2012)

How to Be an Adult in Faith and Spirituality (Paulist Press, 2011)

Daring to Trust: Opening Ourselves to Real Love and Intimacy
(Shambhala Publications, 2010)

Being True to Life: Poetic Paths to Personal Growth
(Shambhala Publications, 2009)

Making Love Last: How to Sustain Intimacy and Nurture Genuine Connection
(Shambhala Audio, 2008)

Wisdom's Way: Quotations for Contemplation (Human Development Books, 2008)

When the Past Is Present: Healing the Emotional Wounds That Sabotage Our
Relationships (Shambhala Publications, 2008)

The Power of Coincidence: How Life Shows Us What We Need to Know
(Shambhala Publications, 2007)

The Sacred Heart of the World: Restoring Mystical Devotion
to Our Spiritual Life (Paulist Press, 2007)

Mary Within Us: A Jungian Contemplation of Her Titles and Powers
(Human Development Books, 2007)

The Five Things We Cannot Change: And the Happiness We Find
by Embracing Them (Shambhala Publications, 2005)

How to Be an Adult in Relationships: The Five Keys to Mindful Loving
(Shambhala Publications, 2002), also available as an
audiobook (Shambhala Audio, 2013)

Shadow Dance: Liberating the Power and Creativity of Your Dark Side
(Shambhala Publications, 1999)

When Love Meets Fear: Becoming Defense-less and Resource-full
(Paulist Press, 1997)

How to Be an Adult: A Handbook for Psychological and Spiritual Integration
(Paulist Press, 1991)

The Power of Grace

*Recognizing Unexpected
Gifts on Our Path*

DAVID RICHO

Shambhala
Boston & London
2014

Shambhala Publications, Inc.
Horticultural Hall
300 Massachusetts Avenue
Boston, Massachusetts 02115
www.shambhala.com

9 8 7 6 5 4 3 2 1

First Edition
Printed in the United States of America

♾ This edition is printed on acid-free paper that meets the
American National Standards Institute Z39.48 Standard.
♻ This book is printed on 30% postconsumer recycled paper.
For more information please visit www.shambhala.com.

Distributed in the United States by Penguin Random House LLC
and in Canada by Random House of Canada Ltd

Library of Congress Cataloging-in-Publication Data

Richo, David, 1940–
The power of grace: recognizing unexpected gifts
on our path / David Richo.—First edition.
pages   cm
ISBN 978-1-61180-146-0 (alk. paper)
1. Grace (Theology)—Miscellanea. I. Title.
BT769.R53 2014
202'.117—dc23
2013048270

To all the people I have worked with at Shambhala
during these fifteen years:
Warm thanks and deep bows
for giving me the chance
to share what came to me by grace

Contents

Introduction

"Suddenly, the perfect solution just popped into my mind."

"I don't know where I found the courage, but I spoke up."

"I can't, for the life of me, figure out how it happened, but everything just fell into place."

"I have practiced my art since childhood, but I know there are moments when I go way beyond my skill level."

"Finally, without even trying, I met just the right guy or woman."

"I don't know what came over me, but after all of these years of hanging back, I finally stepped up to the plate."

"I felt as if I were somehow guided to this decision."

"It was a moment of truth."

"The realization came to me in a dream."

"While volunteering at hospice I have found myself sometimes saying something really right on, and I know I did not think of it on my own or know it before."

"I just stopped wanting to retaliate. Somehow, I had a change of heart and was able to forgive."

We have all said things like this and have wondered where the "special gift" came from. We have found out, again and again, that more seems to be going on in our life than can be accounted for by our own efforts or our own level of knowledge. We keep noticing that something more is afoot in the world than just ourselves and what we do. Our forward move on life's path does not seem to be based solely on our accomplishments, merit, or our sense of worthiness. Something seems to be helping us, an empowering force around us that yet seems to be within us.

If we look back over the episodes and milestones of our lives, we notice that often something beneficial was happening that was not the result of our choice, effort, or expectation. We were somehow guided to or given an impetus to make a leap into something new. That special assistance, unearned, unforeseen, unplanned, often unnoticed, is a description of grace, the gift dimension of life.

The experience of grace makes the world less scary. We feel that we have more to rely on than only our own ego as we face life's most menacing threats and buffets. Trust in grace is an antidote to fear of what life may bring, because it enables us to feel that we have something going for us in any predicament.

"Call upon the Force!" Luke Skywalker, in *Star Wars,* takes this advice. If he is to achieve success, it will not depend on his skills alone. There is something else, and it is reliable, something he cannot conjure but can only call upon. It is from the universe, but it is in him too. This is grace, the invisible star of his—and of every human's—story.

The Force is with Luke because he is important to the galaxy—just as we are. This book is about the Force—grace—that is with us so that we too can fulfill our destiny.

But Luke also noticed that the Force was not enough. He knew that he would have to contribute his own ingenuity and perseverance in order to fulfill his challenging task. Grace is not meant to do it all. Grace is a gift, but it recruits our effort so we can join in the enterprise. Grace gives us an opportunity; it is up to us to step up to the plate. This can mean acting with courage when the going gets rough. It can mean taking hold and holding on when the time has come to persevere. To know the difference is itself a grace.

Our life is thus a combination of what comes to us unbidden and what we choose to do in response. So, for instance, it is the grace of synchronicity, a meaningful coincidence, that leads us to meet a suitable partner at just the right moment. This simply happens. Then it is up to us to form and nurture a meaningful relationship. We commit ourselves to continue the venture that grace began.

Thus, grace is both a comfort and a challenge. We are comforted by the invisible incentive that kicks in for us, giving us the sense that something helpful is at our side. Yet we are also challenged by the next steps we will be asked to take to follow up on the opportunity being offered to us. For instance, we find contentment in discovering the career that fits for us, but it will be a challenge to take the laborious steps to make a success of it.

Our sense of our own wholeness would be diminished if all there were in life was what we do—with no room for grace to join in on the playing out of our story. Our world would be sadly deficient if everything depended on us, with no surprising benefits landing in our laps unexpectedly and unpredictably. It is a joy to realize that our world is a web of life that combines do-it-yourself activity with a vast network of unseen assistance.

We might feel the coming of grace into our lives as a caring about us from a power beyond us. We interpret this sense of being held or cared about as evidence of a friendly universe. We come to trust that something wants us to find fulfillment, happiness, and enlightenment—just what we want for each other when we love. We feel an unexpected alliance between ourselves and the universe or a power higher than our ego. This is connection, accompaniment, the essence of love. We recall Socrates's words in Plato's *Symposium:* "Human nature will not easily find a helper better than love."

For some of us, family members and friends who were dear to us and have died sometimes seem to be present to us in an accompanying way. Since accompaniment is a quality of grace, we can say that their life was a grace to us. Their giving to us did not end with their demise; it goes on. We may carry a felt sense that somehow those who loved us and whom we loved so much did not abandon us totally but live in our hearts in a companionable, sometimes guiding way. When this is our actual experience, no one can convince us otherwise.

In any case, in a moment of grace we understand that we are not alone. There is something or someone reaching into our saga and participating in how our evolution progresses. We can learn to notice the graces in our life story. Eventually, we can learn to see that something, we know not what and beyond our control, is enlarging us and multiplying our options. The "something" is not some *thing* but rather an energy, a force, an operative principle in people, places, and things. Paul Davies, a theoretical physicist, approaches this same point in his book *Accidental Universe:* "Extraordinary physical coincidences and apparently accidental cooperation . . . offer compelling evidence that something is going on. . . . A hidden principle seems to be at work, organizing the universe in a coherent way." The word *hidden* reminds me now that all the words about grace in this book are metaphors, crude and inexact, for a mysterious encounter with forces that hold and aid us.

Grace is not a concept found in a psychology book, seldom even in a book of spiritual practices. It calls to us from the realizations of mystics and, of course, from our own experience, which feels trustworthy to us no matter how outlandish it may seem to the world of science. Our experience has to be the final arbiter of our personal truth.

Yet we also know that grace is an ancient belief in the human psyche, as old as religion and history. Socrates opposed the doctrine of the Sophists that *arête,* that is, virtue, can be learned or earned. He showed that moral excellence was more a gift of the gods than the result of parental nurture or personal effort. This gift is what we are referring to as grace.

A careful reading of early literature, for example the *Iliad* and the *Odyssey,* reveals that every achievement, wisdom, or virtue of a hero is ascribed to the help/grace of a god or goddess. The alternative is hubris, the arrogant belief that we humans are *it,* that our own skills are all that is required for success. This inflated-ego style is what catapults the hero into a tragic downfall. With increasing spiritual consciousness, humans come to see that grace, and awareness of it with thanks for it, is the royal road to the deposing of our solitary ego from its stone throne in our psyches. This is how opening to grace is a spiritual victory.

We see an example of how grace dismantles the ego in 12-step recovery programs. The addict comes to see his powerlessness over his cravings and is moved to rely on a power beyond his ego. Then a transition occurs that can only be accounted for by grace: the style of the addict, "I want more for me," becomes the style of recovery: "There is *more* with me."

On its own, the ego does not want to surrender to a power described as greater than itself, no matter how helpful it is. This is why grace is called amazing, as in the famous hymn. It can successfully compel the most stubborn force on earth, the arrogant ego, to surrender to the truth that it is not really in control and to become humble enough to ask for help. Grace is thus also the help that leads to help.

The word *grace* is usually associated with religion and belief in God. This book is not about theology but about how we can take a concept from religion and appreciate what it can offer for our own spiritual and personal progress. We can find an enriching resource, an archetypal reality, within the religious tradition that has preserved a belief in grace over the centuries. That is what is so exciting—and promising—about our topic.

Indeed, so many realities have to wait until the world is ready to make them fully understandable or acceptable. Here is an analogy: Science fiction proposes fantasies that might someday be realities. Heroes and explorers accomplish feats that might someday be common practice, for example, flight across the Atlantic. Likewise, religion preserves beliefs that are insights into the purposes and powers of humanity.

It seems to me that anyone can notice and respond to a gift dimension in life, with or without a belief in God. A higher power does not necessarily need to be identified with a traditional view of God. It does not even have to have a name. A higher power can be an interior dimension of our psyche, transcendent because it's beyond what ego can muster or master. The transcendent is the *more* that cannot be grasped by intelligence, only by experience. It can be felt fully but not fully understood intellectually. It is like the love felt in a favor, like the awe felt in nature. We recall John Muir in *My First Summer in the Sierra:* "It is easier to feel than to realize, or in any way explain, Yosemite grandeur."

With or without religion, any of us can believe in—and most of us have noticed—a resource beyond our own will or intellect that helps us on our path. This is grace, a power that is beyond our control or ability to predict, something beyond mere chance, something that blesses us beyond our ability to bless ourselves. This is the sense in which I will use the word *transcendent* in the pages that follow. Once we notice and acknowledge the workings of grace in our daily experience, we begin to see it as an underlying element in all that happens and an indispensable feature of human growth.

Grace is a given of life. An acknowledgment of grace does nothing less than widen our vision of what it really means to be human. The destiny we are called to, our true fulfillment, is transcendent, beyond mere survival, the *more* than what we thought possible. We can only come to it with an aptitude for immense surprise:

More is present here than just you and me.

More happens than what we make happen.

More is afoot than what we see in front of us.

To find our full humanity we need contact with more than the minimum criteria defined as mental health in Psychology 101: self-esteem, effective relationships, and acting responsibly at work and in society. We see this most clearly in the fact that we were given organs that we still don't know how to make the most of, for example, mind, heart, genitals. We certainly need more than scientific or medical information to activate them to their full extent. Likewise, our spiritual calling to cocreate a world of justice, peace, and love is too grand an enterprise to accomplish by willpower alone. If we have imaginations that can reach such goals and we cannot achieve them entirely on our own, it must be that we require transcendent assistance if we are ever to evolve fully.

If we had to accomplish goals that we were innately incapable of and there were no grace to supplement our inadequacy, then life would be a heartless joke and despair our only option. That would contradict the inexorable and everywhere-visible fact that a forward-moving evolution is the design and direction of all that is—with no being excluded, especially not us. In fact, one way we know that grace is at work is that it moves us. Indeed, ever-advancing evolution is its most prominent purpose.

It is not stretching a point to say that our appreciation of grace is an essential element not only of spirituality but also of our relationships with one another and with the world. Indeed, there is a direct connection between grace and how we see our life purpose. If our purpose is to become wealthy or controlling for our own aggrandizement, there is no need for grace, only effort and luck. If our purpose is to become abundantly humane, we will feel the need for grace every day.

Evolution is the story of how nature keeps unfolding. Thus, it is about the *more,* since it is continually transcending what was for what will be. From birth onward, beings seek to do more than survive and reproduce. They strive to develop their creativity and to find fulfillment beyond their immediate needs. In other words, we are all continually attempting to transcend ourselves. That yearning originates in the spiritual dimension of life, where grace abides. To use a familiar personification, grace is the guardian angel escorting us over many bridges, rickety or smooth, over waters troubled or tranquil. We were given a lifetime just so we could make those crossings with grace.

Our sense of and trust in the assisting force of grace influences our view of how we and the world work. In fact, grace is a decisive element in our ability to approach the puzzling questions that have intrigued humanity all of these centuries. An acknowledgment of transcendent grace makes us more friendly toward questions like Why are we here? Why is there suffering? What does it take to be happy? What will happen to us after death? Once we have acknowledged the reality of grace, we more easily say yes to these mysteries rather than insisting on knowing "Why?" The whys turn to ashes in the fire of grace, the something, we know not what, always at work to make us more than we are now and to make the world more than it is yet. All of these "mores" make the whys less and less urgent.

I told a friend, Ron, I was working on a book on grace and received this response: "I believe in miracles, but I do not count on miracles. I do, somehow and in some way, believe in grace, and I do count on it. I just seem to have this idea that grace is looming on my shoulder and knows exactly what to do when I am struggling or clueless. Somehow, it just knows when to enter my life, and I can't control it, I can only trust that grace is my 'Wing Man.' It does not guarantee my safety or joy or whatever, it just lets me know that there is something bigger than myself that is very kind and all-knowing and that if my landing field is properly maintained (by myself preparing to receive grace), it may just land in my field of life. Grace is a gift, and when I get such a gift, I get a very good feeling of being valued and appreciated."

It has been a great grace to me to write this book. It has not been a task but an opening. I am hoping it will be a grace and opening to you as you read it. All it will take is a yes to the *more*—and who would say no to that?

> I don't know who—or what—put the question; I don't know when it was put. I don't even remember answering. But at some moment I did answer *Yes* to Someone—or something.
>
> —DAG HAMMARSKJÖLD, *Markings*

1

What Is Grace?

There's a divinity that shapes our ends
Rough-hew them how we will.
—WILLIAM SHAKESPEARE, *Hamlet*

A torn meniscus brought me to a knee surgeon. When I asked him about my prognosis, he replied in this mirthful but provocative way: "The success of the operation depends on three elements: my skill as a surgeon, your fidelity to the physical therapy program, and the beneficence of the knee gods." He said that last phrase with a twinkle in his eye. I smiled too and knew what he meant by knee gods. He was referring to the mysterious and arbitrary variable in any healing process. This is the realm of the uncaused, unpredictable, and yes, haphazard—what I see as beyond our human powers. It is called grace when it brings a positive result, immediately or later.

Grace is defined in the dictionary in a variety of ways. It can mean rhythmic or refined movement; courteous goodwill; a prayer of gratitude before meals; an appealing form of etiquette or polite behavior, as in social graces.

Grace can also refer to an elegant resignation to a negative event: "He accepted his defeat with the best possible grace." The art of a "graceful exit" adds the note of wise timing. "Grace under pressure" is handling stress with resilience and equanimity. We also say: "He fell from grace" when we mean that someone fell out of favor with a group or individual.

The dictionary introduces us to the element of mystery when it gives the theological meaning of grace as "a gratuitous favor from God or a divinely granted blessing." This form of grace, beyond cause and effect, that we cannot generate, but only receive. Such grace can come through to us as sudden or gradual access to wisdom or healing beyond what our minds or bodies can produce on their own. Grace also arrives in the form of meaningful chance. This is synchronicity, a coincidence or correlation that proves to be significant in our life.[*]

When this transcendent grace comes to us, we feel gratitude. We might then say: "That was a blessing" or "It was a miracle." We might feel a sense of being specially accompanied or safeguarded because the grace seems to be a personal favor, a sign of being cared about by a source beyond our ego.

Graces that transcend our skills and powers can be described as favorable conditions. Things come together in just such a way as to benefit or expand us. We discover unexpected resources such as these:

- A series of coincidences ferries us to a significant relationship or a gratifying career.
- We have a hunch that leads to a life-changing truth or plan.
- We gain a sudden insight that is "Beyond the Art to Earn," as Emily Dickinson wrote.
- We accomplish what can't be accounted for if all we have going for us is our limited level of skill.
- We gain advantages that exceed the exertions we have expended.

---

[*] Throughout this book I expand upon the themes of my book *The Power of Coincidence* (Shambhala Publications, 2007), which treats the subject of synchronicity in detail.

It is also true that we contain potentials of strength and wisdom within us but not necessarily the probability that they will activate. Grace is what grants probability. By grace we are given an opportunity. Then it is up to us to use it for growth and good. In fact, life itself is a grace because all that happens, without exception, presents us with an opportunity for evolution and enlightenment.

Grace is also a gift with momentum. Grace is not a gift we own but a gift in movement, that is, a gift with incentive to move us and move through us. It does not land on us like rain. It blows through us like a wind and is meant to reach everyone else too. It is a moving event that wants to keep moving through us to the world around us and vice versa.

Grace is thus mobile in ways like these:

- Grace moves us to act, to change, to grow, to love more and in ever-new ways.
- Grace cannot be owned or hoarded. We receive and pass grace on. Grace is a constant exchange coming to us, only to move through us, as in the example of the parent speaking wisely and kindly to his child, who someday will speak that way to her child.
- Grace moves through experiences, events, predicaments, people, places, and things. They are not sources of grace but conduits through which graces come to us.

Grace is not an ontological entity. We are seeing that it is active, experiential, fertile, creative, mobile, vibrant, erotic, celebratory, transformational. Grace is like an electrical charge that activates us and everything around us through us. Grace can come in the form of a lively and mobilizing event that moves us and then, through us, can transform our hearts, our lifestyle, our relationships. Any person, place, thing, feeling, thought, or event can be a means of transporting the transcendent into our lives. More can always come from everywhere and everyone. As Emily Dickinson says: "Contained in this short life / Are magical extents."

How Do We Know It Is Grace?

We can now understand grace as an unearned benefit from a transcendent source meant for a psychological or spiritual purpose.

We can take this basic definition phrase by phrase to see the criteria by which we can know whether an event or realization in our life might be a grace:

"Unearned" means that it is not the result of action, effort, or merit on our part. Grace is pure gift.

"Transcendent source" is a mysterious, that is, unknowable and unexplainable, power or force that is beyond—that transcends—human making, natural causes, or purely random chance. But even though these three cannot cause grace, they can be channels of grace: Human actions and the wonders of nature can be vehicles of grace when they help us move along on our spiritual path. Chance can be a channel of grace when it is not mere random coincidence but something that is recognizably meaningful—something that makes a difference in our lives in a long-lasting and purposeful way.

A "psychological purpose" is fulfillment of ourselves by freely and unashamedly being who we really are and living in accord with our deepest needs, values, and wishes.

A "spiritual purpose" refers to what is beneficial for our evolving toward our destiny: Our personal destiny is to fulfill ourselves by showing all the love we have, acting wisely, and making the most of our talents. Our collective destiny is to share our gifts for the good of all beings and to cocreate a world of justice, peace, and love. This happens when we feel a shift deep in ourselves from primitive ways of behaving, for example, infighting, to a more evolved style, cooperating. In that sense, grace is how the story of evolution happens within an individual.

With these criteria in mind, we can summarize how to assess whether what has happened to us or is happening now is a grace:

1. Was this or will this turn out to be ultimately beneficial?
2. Did this come from beyond my ego, something I could not make happen by producing, earning, or meriting it?

3. Did this have a meaning and purpose that help me manifest my inner wholeness psychologically or spiritually? Does this shift me into a higher consciousness than my ego could have reached on its own?

Number 1 describes grace as a gift.
Number 2 describes grace as transcendent.
Number 3 describes grace as a guide to our fulfillment and our destiny.

> We normally think of history as one catastrophe after another . . . narratives of human pain, assembled in sequence. . . . But history is also the narratives of grace, the recountings of those blessed and inexplicable moments when someone did something for someone else, saved a life, bestowed a gift, gave something beyond what was required by circumstance.
>
> —THOMAS CAHILL

Grace and Graces

We can distinguish ongoing grace from specific or occasional graces:

Grace is, first, the built-in continuous gift that comes to all of us from life and nature. The fact that we go on living is grace. The fact that there is a world still swirling through space is grace. We are thus all always and everywhere the recipients of grace.

Graces, on the other hand, are immediate, sudden, impromptu, ad hoc gifts we receive only sometimes. For instance, as we saw at the beginning of the introduction, we sometimes suddenly come up with an intuition or show an uncharacteristic courage that we know we did not have before. We realize that something has arisen in us that exceeds our ordinary powers. In other words, we have more going for us than we ever dared imagine. The *more* is more than what ego usually does, as in the following example: We may be surprised to find ourselves talking to our child in an unusually wise and skillful way. We are showing a caring connection—love—by our words and manner. We are being respectful and encouraging, perhaps quite unlike what was modeled to us as children by our own parents. We wonder where such well-timed skill came from. In that moment, our baser self—the habit-driven ego that repeats the past and can be punitive or unfeeling—was off duty. Instead, the voice of a higher self than ego came through, the voice of grace within us.

Ongoing grace is a continuum of favor toward us. It is an animating power that remains no matter what. Grace is never not happening. For instance, an inborn gift or talent that remains with us throughout our life can be identified as grace—though we may not always access it. The grace of being loved has been, is, and will be happening all of our life—though we may not always notice it. The grace of enlightenment is in our very nature all the time—though it takes a special grace to access freedom from the fear, craving, and delusion that hold it hostage.

Occasional graces are instances in which we find more than we could have imagined possible in ourselves or others in the ordinary course of events. The occasion shows us that we know more than it should have been possible for us to know. There are also times when we accomplish more than could have been shaped by any talent or virtue we were aware of. Examples of specific graces include unusual opportunities, advantages, advances, reinforcements, supports, enhancements, inspirations, intuitions, healings, rescues, liberations, empowerments. For instance, in a physically abusive relationship, a partner might find in therapy just the support that can help her separate. A young person who is confused about what career path to take may meet someone who introduces him to a line of work that fits his talents and interests perfectly. Someone embroiled in family complications may suddenly know exactly how to bring about a peaceful solution for everyone.

Continuous grace, ongoing help, is like the electrical current in our home: it is constantly on. Graces are like activations of the current for particular lamps. The only difference is that when it comes to grace, we are not the ones who throw the switch. We simply receive the burst of light. Using another example, our hand is not playing the piano. Our hand is only the instrument for a larger and deeper creative reality that is coming through. A character in Thomas Bernhard's novel *The Loser* goes so far as to say: "The ideal piano player is the one who wants to be the piano."

All of evolution is an example of the combination of grace and graces. The enduring grace of nature supports our life on the planet from birth to death. All the movements in the universe cohere in one ongoing continuity of grace. This grace ignites all that is and all that happens. Natural evolution then proceeds through a series of discrete graces, gradual upgrades, and quantum leaps. The Big Bang was the first grace. The new insights that came to us today are our most recent graces.

> I know there is a truth that cannot be thought, only received.
> —TRACY COCHRAN, "THE NIGHT I DIED"

Three Arrivals of Grace

We pay attention to heroic-journey stories because they tell us about the landscape of our own deep—unconscious—purposes and longings. They depict the shape our own story can take. This follows from the fact that hero stories have similar themes and characters in all cultures and in every century. They therefore reflect archetypal energies— recurrent motifs about the meaning of our common human destiny. Luke Skywalker's and every hero's mission in the galaxy is ours; only the names and dates are changing.

There are three specific arrivals of graces in hero stories. Graces come at the beginning, middle, and end of the journey. This is a metaphor for how graces are geared to initiate, support, and complete us on our own journey. We can rely on those three activations of grace in the course of our lives, but we cannot predict how or when they will manifest.

There is a grace that helps us get started on the path to enlightenment, wisdom, and love. There is a grace that supports and sustains us as we walk the path. There is a grace that expands the reaching of our goal into the discovering of our destiny. A goal is an aim we know and plan for; a destiny is a fulfillment beyond anything we could have imagined.

Grace is a guide when it helps us begin something in life, a companion when it moves us along, and a fulfiller when it makes completion possible. We can use an example: Grace as a guide, in the form of a sick person, an old person, and a dead person, initiated Gautama's journey from his father's palace to becoming a buddha, an enlightened teacher. Grace, in the forms of companions, helped him advance to his goal. Grace, in the form of his awakening under the fig tree, helped him fulfill himself. Grace enriched the outcome of the story when the Buddha found more than his goal of personal enlightenment, what he had wanted. Instead, he found his collective destiny to bring enlightenment to the world, what we all needed.

Indeed, in every hero story the hero finds *more* than he ever hoped for at the beginning of his journey. The true goal of the journey is unknown because our ego cannot easily imagine how great a gift is coming to us. The protagonist becomes the heroine when she discovers the bigness of grace—and of what is within her. Here are some familiar examples of this feature of the heroic journey story:

Hero/Heroine	Original Goal	What the Person Actually Found in Addition
Percival	Find the Holy Grail	The realization that wholeness is within, not outside, himself
Robin Hood	Feed the poor with money from the rich	Maid Marian, his soul mate
Harriet Tubman	Escape from slavery	The ability to help others toward freedom
Helen Keller	Learn to communicate	Skill as a speaker and author that made it possible for her to give encouragement to others

Anne Frank	Write of her experiences	A way to help others understand suffering and gain hope
Rosa Parks	Assert her right to sit anywhere on the bus	The opportunity to inspire others to initiate a civil rights movement
Martin Luther King Jr.	Launch a national civil rights movement	The satisfaction of seeing federal laws change
Dorothy in Oz	Return home to Kansas	Her own inner power, finding out that home is within herself
Luke Skywalker	Contribute to the safety of the galaxy	His own connection to the dark side and the Force, both within himself
	Our self-designed goals might be based on a limited imagination.	*Here we access a resource beyond our own usual limitations, and our imagination opens abundantly.*

How do the three occasions of grace—beginning, middle, and end—work in our own lives?

Initiating graces come to all of us at threshold times when we move into something that is new and life changing. Initiation as a change of status is sometimes ritualized in an initiatory ritual. This is meant to be an opening to grace. (When the grace dimension is lacking, an initiation might be only superficial or, worse, a hazing.)

Advancing graces are boosting and bolstering. They grant us a quantum leap forward in our projects, beyond our own skill or power to effect.

Completing graces take us beyond what we can finish on our own. For instance, in "America the Beautiful," Katharine Lee Bates wrote:

O beautiful for heroes proved
In liberating strife.

Who more than self their country loved . . .

. . . .

America! America!
God shed his grace on thee
And crown thy good with brotherhood . . .

These lyrics confidently assert that, because of grace, our giving of
our lives for freedom can be "crowned," that is, topped with, added to,
brought into a finale of brotherly unity. We can't do that part on our
own no matter how much courage we show. How ironic that the next
line shows an *incompletion:* "From sea to shining sea" includes only
the continental United States in the brotherhood, not the whole world.
When will we ever ask for more than what the limited imagination is
satisfied with? When will we dare ask for *all* that grace can shed on us?

Spiritual practice follows the same threefold outline as in journey
stories: a move initiated in us by grace, then our daring to walk the path
by the help of accompanying grace, and finally any further develop-
ments as grace fulfills and completes us.

Buddhism uses the threefold motif found in mythic stories in its
teaching about the Three Excellences or Three Noble Principles. A
summary of them is presented by the fourteenth-century Tibetan
teacher Longchenpa: "Begin with bodhichitta [turning toward enlight-
enment], do the main practice without concepts, conclude by dedicat-
ing the merit to the welfare of all beings. These, together and complete,
are the three vital supports for progressing on the path to liberation."
The term *vital supports* is a beautiful description of grace.

Buddhism offers practices that show how to cultivate the Three
Excellences:

1. To encourage an initiating grace, we make an altruistic intention to bring an enlightened consciousness into our relationships to others.
2. During the practice of mindfulness, we abide in continual
   awareness of the inherent interdependence of all things. We

keep reminding ourselves that we are not acting separately, that we are not separate.

3. Upon completion of mindfulness practice, we dedicate our virtue and change to the benefit not only of ourselves and those we love but of all beings. Awakening is thus altruistic, not self-centered. And it is grace that leads to our awakening to universal love.

Finally, we see a striking similarity between the three forms of graces we have been describing and a common religious teaching. The Holy Spirit is believed to be at once the originator, sustaining power, and final goal of the evolving world—containing in itself the same three dimensions of grace we meet in hero stories. The "assisting force" that appears at the beginning, middle, and end of the journey is another name for Spirit at work in the story of us and of the universe. This is referred to in theology as an "indwelling divine presence," not something far away from us. (Nothing is far away from us.)

What Is Transcendence?

Since grace is gratuitous, not based on merit, it is wildly autonomous and unpredictable. These factors can be disconcerting to the ego that wants to be in control, to maintain order, to know what to expect, and to place everything in well-defined categories.

When we acknowledge that favors come to us from a higher power than our ego, we are acknowledging a mystery dimension in our lives. This is contact with the transcendent. Then we are more likely to see the necessity of grace as a crucial supplement to our limited ego powers, and we welcome it. The journey archetype built into every human psyche gives us optimism because an empowering assistance comes to every hero and heroine. An archetype is a specific energy, orientation, or purpose that appears as a recurring symbol in human consciousness and stories.

We are now ready to look more deeply into what is meant by *transcendence*. Transcendence does not imply a split between spirit and matter. The transcendent is not about spirit's being superior to matter. Actually, everything has a transcendent dimension. Here are some examples:

- Our bodies are transcendent when they are present in and for the community of our fellow humans rather than for ourselves alone.
- Our interior depth knowledge transcends our logical thinking when we make room for the imaginal.
- Our sexual desire transcends our ego when it seeks union with others through but not limited to our bodies.
- Our love is transcendent when it takes us beyond our near and dear and extends to all beings far and wide so we can cocreate a world of justice, peace, and love.
- Our generosity is transcendent when we give more than is asked of us or more than what is required of us.

Our references to what is beyond ego—like our references to grace—are not meant to be dualistic. For instance, transcendence doesn't leave behind or invalidate that which it transcends. Thus, when our love transcends its scope from our near and dear to all beings, we still love our near and dear. Likewise, transcendence is not to be construed as dualistic, since, as we have been seeing, it can refer to what is deep within us rather than far above us. Chapter 4 of *Alcoholics Anonymous* states: "We found the Great Reality deep down within us. In the last analysis it is only there that He may be found." The "deep down" usually refers to the unconscious in the human psyche, what gives birth to new myths, new revelations, new paradigms, new discoveries, new ways of living and loving. Perhaps another term for *higher power* would be *deeper power*.

To transcend is not to reject or dismiss the full spectrum of anything real; that would be impossible. Transcendence is an emergent property of our being. Transcending always includes containing, holding what is so that its richest potential can emerge. Indeed, the transcendent can be more like a container of all reality, a field in which we live rather than something or someone in a sky above us. As we let go of dualistic think-ing, we open ourselves to paradox. Then we behold the world in which apparent opposites combine. We see how they can become friendly with each other, complement each other. In the world of paradox, noth-ing is incompatible, nothing is exiled, opposites unite. This is not new information for us. We accommodated it long ago. Earlier in childhood than we can remember, we heard or sang these words from Phillips Brooks's 1865 carol, "O Little Town of Bethlehem": "In thy dark streets shineth the everlasting light."

No effort of ours can collapse polarities into unities; it simply hap-pens. It is a gift. Thus, the link that unites seeming opposites is grace, the deepest of all paradoxes. This is how we no longer see, for instance, a distinction between the sacred and the profane. The ubiquity of the transcendent means that nothing is mundane; all is epiphany-ready. Thus, body and spirit are not mutually exclusive but inter-are. Each of us—and all natural things—is embodied spirit, spiritualized body.

When we say that we transcend our body, we simply mean that we are not compulsively tied to its grossest needs but see how those needs can be vehicles for our evolving spirituality. To transcend is thus to find a potential for evolution in anything or any experience. We do not re-ject anything, only enter it by the door our primitive impulses may have overlooked. We then go beyond while taking with. We see this concept of inclusion in a poem by Izumi Shikibu, a tenth-century Japanese Buddhist poet:

Gazing at the moon as dawn began,
Solitary, center sky,
I knew myself utterly,
Nothing at all was left out.

The poem also shows how the transcendent can appear in an expe-rience of the natural world. In fact, transcendence can refer to the inner depth of nature, what makes it generate new life again and again, what makes it beautiful to behold.

We keep in mind that words like *deep down* and *outer* or *inner* are spatial metaphors, so they do not, of course, do justice to the mystery. The reality is more than words can say. Grace is the gift dimension of life. The transcendent is the *more* dimension. There is something in us and in everything that exceeds our ego and its powers, our intellectual acumen and our willpower.

Transcend in Latin means "climb over." The Latin word for "go beyond," with a similar meaning, is implied in the English word *extravagant*. We become wonderfully extravagant indeed as our sense of scarcity vanishes in the realization that we are rich in graces. *Transcend* is also associated in its literal meaning to *exorbitant,* going "out of this world." We see the concept of transcendence in the word *surpass. Ecstasy* means intense delight, but its literal Greek meaning is "to stand outside." This is a metaphor for breaking out of the narrow limits set by habit and ego, precisely what brings us bliss. According to the Orthodox saint Gregory of Sinai, we are filled with ecstasy in the experience of grace: "The energy of grace is the power of spiritual fire that fills the heart with joy."

Recently I was listening to a radio interview with the rock musician Jack Black. He said he was an atheist but that at certain moments the joy of music gave him "a spiritual experience." It lifted him to a place he knew he could not arrive at on his own. This is a description of the transcendent. We see again that *transcendence* does not have to be a religious word. The grace element is in the fact that we do not "go" beyond but are "taken" beyond our usual limits. Included in any such transcendent, beyond-ego moment is the realization that we did not make it happen but that it was given to us. We don't have to identify the source; it is a power beyond our usual reach. The wonderful thing is that the power *wants* to come through, waits for just the right moment and place.

Transcendent grace seems otherworldly but is, in fact, the world within us that sustains us. Grace shows us our bigness, as Saint Augustine noticed: "I am a changing, multiform life of immense prodigious size." Walt Whitman adds: "I am large, I contain multitudes." This big mind/soul is the higher self, our true nature, who we are beyond our individual ego and personality.

The transcendent action of grace is how the higher self works in the ego world. This is why we feel the special voice of wisdom coming through us rather than from us. Our accessing powers higher than ego can assemble is what is meant by receiving grace.

The transcendent is a context in which we live, one that is more intense than can be guessed by our limited intellects. The transcendent in this sense also takes us beyond our individualism into awareness of the vast web of life. This is why we feel the transcendent in a moment of awe at Mother Nature. The mother energy is a field within, not an intervention from without. That "within" is a context of the transcendent, a context in which human and divine are only one reality.

But what happens when opposites do not combine as only one reality, when, instead, they remain at loggerheads, as in a dilemma? We are faced with two options, both of which are unacceptable. Yet a solution can appear: thesis and antithesis can lead to a synthesis that both combines and transcends them.

Carl Jung likewise spoke of "the transcendent function of the psyche": the tendency of the psyche to produce a "healing third" option when opposites collide. This event is not a synthesis of the opposites but the arrival of an altogether new possibility. A healing image, solution, or realization arises in a dream or by a sudden intuition or in an experience of synchronicity. Something has come through that we could not have conjured by thought—another example of how grace reaches us as an unexpected gift.

The More That We Are

> I am larger, better than I thought,
> I did not know I held so much goodness.
> —WALT WHITMAN,
> "SONG OF THE OPEN ROAD"

In the loving-kindness practice we aspire to show beneficent caring and heartfelt goodwill to ourselves, to those who are dear to us, to those who have no claim on us, to those who do not please us, to those who may not like us, and finally to all beings. It is a gift of grace to reach this universal level of loving-kindness, and our fidelity to our practice keeps opening us to it. In addition, the practice frees us from dualism since it confers love equally on everyone, without rank, priority, or division.

Spiritual practices open us to accessing the love, wisdom, and compassion always and already in our true nature. But grace is the transcendent *more* that enriches those three qualities so they can open and deepen in our lives. Grace makes our love unconditional, our wisdom oracular, our compassion universal. These add up to a life purpose that seeks more than minimal growth: We want to become generous caretakers not only of ourselves and those around us but of the planet. We become committed to forming a world of justice, peace, and love. That widening of our perspective and commitment cannot be accounted for only by our spiritual practices, no matter how fervently we pursue them. We have something going for us that exceeds any result a practice can cause. Something has kicked in to swell the depth and scope of our virtues.

Here is an example of expanding our compassion so that it becomes universal. Feel-good compassion happens when we feel pity only for those whose pain has tugged at our hearts. That is an ego response, since it is based on what *we* find suitable for compassion. When compassion transcends ego, that is, has opened to grace, it is focused on suffering itself, no matter who is feeling it. This is unconditional compassion.

The Roman philosopher Seneca said: "If you want to imitate the gods, bestow your gifts on the ungrateful, for the sun also rises on the wicked and the sea is open even to pirates." We feel compassion equally for those who touch us and for those who disgust us, for friend and enemy, for victim and perpetrator. Our compassion comes from beyond ego preferences; how we show our compassion, however, will be a choice made by our healthy ego: we might hold a victim and confront or simply pray for a perpetrator.

Grace also fills out or expands on what we do in any area of life and how we impact others. For instance, I have noticed in my teaching and writing that people will thank me for how useful or helpful something I said turned out to be. When I hear their version of my comment, I know I did not go as far or as deep as they are quoting. Something alive and aware in them complemented what I said. I gave 50 percent and they received 100 percent. Grace added to my contribution.

We all notice there is more wisdom in us than can be accounted for by the schools we attended, more to our love than what was modeled in our family or past relationships. We have been gaining from sources beyond the sum of all we have learned and experienced. Something has come through to us in insightful moments, from admirable people, surprising realizations, sudden intuitions, startling epiphanies, and unexpected alliances. That something enlarged our capacities for love and wisdom. It is the gift dimension of experience, the grace of *more* in what seemed so limited.

The word *dimension,* as I'm using it, refers to an intangible component or element, for instance, "There is an element of humor in the story." *Dimension* can refer to a felt sense: "Somehow I felt welcome there." Every reality and experience has dimensions beyond those that can be measured. For instance, in a field of poppies we can know the colors and height of each plant. But they also have other dimensions not immediately evident: medicinal use, a quality of inspiration that may help us later when we feel glum, a here-and-now mysteriousness too evocative for words. *More* refers to the transcendent as that which comes into play from beyond human making, natural causes, or random chance—what we know as grace.

Mature spirituality is an opening to the gift dimension of human existence. In other words, spiritual powers are present on every page of our story. We have no power over them, nor can we summon them at will. They come when they are needed, not when we demand them. Our trust, then, is not only in our skills, will, or effort but in the assurance that a force beyond ego or intellect will take effect to help us. The word *beyond* does not place spirituality in a category separate from daily life. It makes all that happens and all that we do one single experience of grace-filled living. By grace the beyond is the within. By grace this passing moment is all there is. By grace this flawed body-mind is wholeness.

Carl Jung, in *Psychology and Alchemy,* wrote: "It is conceivable that by intense effort a person may catch a fleeting glimpse of his own wholeness, accompanied by the feeling of grace, which always characterizes this experience." We can muse that the "feeling of grace" *is* a glimpse of our wholeness. This *more* than ego is the source of grace. More gives more, as Shakespeare implies in *The Winter's Tale:* "It is a surplus of your grace." That surplus is what places effort beside, not instead of, grace.

On the evening after writing the preceding paragraph I was struck by a commercial on TV for an emergency alert system. An older man is shown falling in his living room and calling for help. No one can hear him, so he lies there, helpless and despondent, for a whole day. In the next scene he is shown, with a smile, after he has purchased the alert device. The commercial then cuts to a team of people with phones responding to calls from customers far and wide. The commercial ended with these words from the disabled senior: "With this around my neck at all times, I will never be alone again." I wondered to what extent our technology, though undoubtedly helpful, has reduced our sense of transcendent powers or the need for them. As technology makes life more secure, what happens to our trust in grace? I mused then on how the world has changed since the time of King David, who had no one to rely on in the dark valley but the Good Shepherd.

> If danger was around me, as the mysterious communication intimated, how could I learn its nature, or the means of averting it, but by meeting my unknown counselor, to whom I could see no reason for imputing any other than kind intentions.
>
> —SIR WALTER SCOTT, *Rob Roy*

2

How Effort Fits In

Spirituality is caught not taught.

—PRAVRAJIKA VRAJAPRANA, *Vedanta: A Simple Introduction*

When someone gives us a gift, we ideally show gratitude and then take the time and effort to put the gift to its best use. Likewise when we receive a grace, we are thankful and we expend effort to put it into practice. A grace within us but without follow-up effort results in the loss of the full fruition of a spiritual opportunity. Dogen Zenji, in his essay "On the Endeavor of the Way" wrote: "Although this inconceivable Dharma [enlightened teaching] is abundant in each person, it is not actualized without practice."

Grace is a transcendence-produced force; effort is an accomplishment-producing force. Effort and grace can work together synergistically. Yet grace does not exist alongside effort in a dualistic way. It is the force that expands the power and effectiveness of our efforts and supports us in continuing them. Psychological work and spiritual practices are examples of our efforts. By them we place a living intention in the universe to stay committed to acting in accord with the graces given to us. Our work and practices may invite further grace. For instance, a grace helps us begin to follow a calling. We put effort into persevering in that calling. Then a new grace supports us in

19

fulfilling our calling. This relay of grace and effort is what makes them synergistic.

Grace is a gift beyond choice and action.

Effort is our choice and action.

Effort comes after and because of grace to make it a lived experience. But grace cannot make effort happen.

Grace may come after effort but not because of it. Effort cannot make grace happen, since it emerges from a transcendent source of power. Saint Teresa of Avila used this garden example to show the connection between effort and grace: She expended effort to draw water from a well or spring to water her garden. But the watering also happened because of rain, "a grace from above." The effort does not cause the rain; it harmoniously complements it.

Here are some examples of the limits of what can be achieved by effort and the unexpected openings that can happen by grace:

We gain knowledge by study and observation; wisdom is a grace, not achieved but received.

We can like and love others; unconditional love is a grace.

We can tolerate hard times; equanimity is a grace.

We can get past our conflicts with people; forgiveness is a grace.

We can endure losing; letting go is a grace.

The metaphor of bread baking works for illustrating how grace follows effort. We have it in us to make and then knead the dough. However, before we put it in the oven, there will be a necessary pause in which it has to rise on its own. The rising is beyond our control or manipulation. All we can do is provide the conditions in which the rising can happen: proper kneading; a cloth covering the bowl; a warm, undisturbed place for it. We cannot produce the rising, we can only wait for it—the equivalent of opening to something. We begin with effort, then suspend it so the next phase can kick in. Grace and effort in bread making, as in life, are not separate but complementary.

Before we move to the next example, we can pause to contemplate this more deeply. The rising of the dough happens in the dark, a metaphor for what happens in us unconsciously and incomprehensibly. The biological term *scotophil* refers to an organism that grows best in darkness. What an optimistic comment on those dark nights when we can't rely on our ego to pull us through.

Now we can look at two examples of how effort is a follow-up to grace. In these instances, we receive a grace that starts us off on a new chapter in our life or produces a deepening of our spirituality. Then effort or practice on our part is necessary to keep it going. For instance, something can move an addict to give up his addiction and enter a program of recovery. Then it will be up to him to practice the twelve steps that move him in that direction. The grace falls flat if it is not followed up by effort, one day at a time.

In Buddhism *bodhicitta* is a turning, a refocusing not conjured by ego, in the direction of enlightenment. Our desire for enlightenment is not caused by any action or intention of ours; it arises on its own. In fact, a common phrase in Buddhist teaching is "the arising of *bodhicitta*." We are moved to appreciate the value of enlightened living as an alcoholic is moved to appreciate the value of sober living. We then engage diligently in spiritual practices that articulate our turn toward enlightenment. This includes mindfulness because enlightenment is awareness of the here and now. It includes loving-kindness because enlightenment is altruistic. Through our practices, but not because of them, *bodhicitta* is continuous, not simply a single initiating moment.

It is remarkable that this turning—in Buddhism and in recovery—leads to a result that is more than personal. In *bodhicitta* our enlightenment is oriented not only toward our own benefit but also toward that of all beings. We wake up for everyone's benefit. It is spiritual altruism. In many spiritual traditions we see this same connection between personal concerns and those of the world. The Hindu teacher Vivekananda, for instance, applied this motto to the Ramakrishna Order: "For one's own spiritual realization and for the good of the world."

The key word *and* in the quotation above reminds us that our concern for our own enlightenment is not like a step that leads to concern for the enlightenment of all beings. Rather, each contains the other. Our move toward self-care or toward the seeking of enlightenment reveals the all-embracing quality of love. We soon notice that caring about others is part of loving ourselves. Love, as the design of the loving-kindness practice illustrates, can't be real if it is limited. It always includes ourselves, others, all others. There is no love of "me only" nor love of "you only." Love is beyond such dualism; it is real only when it is both at once. The grace of love takes no aim but reaches every target.

In 12-step programs, full recovery is likewise not only about stabilizing ourselves but also about caring about the recovery of others. The Twelfth Step of Alcoholics Anonymous is "Having had a spiritual awakening as a result of these steps, we tried to carry this message to alcoholics." The phrase "having had a spiritual awakening" reminds us that something has happened to us, not that something has been done by us. The second phrase, "we tried to carry this message to [other] alcoholics," describes the follow-up practice to the connection between ourselves and others that has already happened. This is how grace meets effort and keeps multiplying.

In both instances—*bodhicitta* and recovery—we respond to grace by putting effort into acting with loving-kindness toward all beings. Grace thus becomes caring connection, love, when it is joined to a practice.

We can describe grace as a shift that happens and effort as a step we take. Our crossing a threshold, our first step, requires grace. A step taken by us follows. This leads to a shift in us that is followed by more steps we take. These can lead to further shifts. Here is what it may look like:

Some force beyond our ego, *bodhicitta*, convinces us of the value of making enlightenment our focus. This is a shift that leads to

Mindfulness, a step we take that leads to

Our opening, a shift that happens in us that leads to

Loving-kindness, a step we take that leads to

Universal compassion, a shift that happens in us.

The same model can be applied to the example of recovery from an addiction. Some force beyond our ego, grace, moves us to make sobriety and recovery our priorities, which leads to

Our joining a program, a step we take that leads to

Our opening, our "getting with the program," a shift that happens in us that leads to

Our working the program, twelve steps we take that lead to

The desire to help other addicts, a shift that happens in us.

We sought our own sobriety, and the gift, the grace of altruism, grew in us. We then made choices to put our altruism into practice, actions we undertake.

In both examples a felt sense of our need for enlightenment or for recovery led to a felt shift, caring about others. This is an example of the grace of finding more than we expected.

> The moment one definitely commits oneself, then providence moves too. A whole stream of events issues from the decision, raising in one's favor all manner of unforeseen incidents, meetings and material assistance, which no man could have dreamt would have come his way.
> —W. H. MURRAY, *The Scottish Himalaya Expedition*

Too Much

Effort shouldn't be the kind of stressful exertion expressed in the saying "no pain no gain." Ease is our style when we respond to grace. The best effort has no compulsion in it. At its best, effort feels like wholeheartedness. Then we may experience gentle fatigue at the end of the day, but it will not have to be exhaustion. We do what we can do, all we can do, and then let things play out as they may. We are not forcing but coaxing, not pushing but prompting. The back and forth between effort and grace is like a dance, not like jackhammering.

We can become obsessed with effort, taxing ourselves, as if our muscle were all we had going for us. Indeed, an excessive accent on effort can indicate a lack of trust in grace as a reliable supplement to our toils. We might also hold ourselves to a standard of accomplishment that is too rigorous for us to achieve without harming ourselves by stress. This can also represent a lack of trust in grace.

The self-help movement has often focused us entirely on improving ourselves. "I need to work on this" makes sense, but not if it means that change and transformation are in our hands only, because then we miss the spiritual dimension.

Likewise, "You make your own reality" disregards the influence and power of other forces, for example, unconscious motivations in how reality takes shape or graces that come to us and point a way. Actually, we can do all the work of processing our experience and dealing with our problems and still fall apart.

When the controlling ego is in the driver's seat, we might ignore the layered texture of reality. We overlook the other dimension of our growth experience, grace. We imagine we are self-made, that we are summed up only by what we accomplish. We are then the little engine that could. Such a belief precludes the need for help from a source beyond our ego. Our psyche is more than just an ego, so more must be needed to complete our program of psychological change and spiritual transformation. Change means acting in a new way. Transformation is complete change, a shift in one's entire being. Change is based on our work on ourselves. Transformation happens only by grace.

Grace may certainly work hand in hand with healthy ego industriousness. Yet it can flower only when our ego surrenders in total openness to the many favors that keep coming to initiate, advance, and crown its exertions. As with dreams, graces don't always give specific information about our path, but they do point to an option or opportunity. Then it is up to us to *live into it* by our openness to what comes next. That style is the opposite of—and a liberation from—excessive concern with effort and seeking. Openness is trust that everything is already and always here.

Our overemphasis on the importance of effort can hark back to childhood. Perhaps we felt compelled to keep doubling our efforts because we imagined that our parents' attention or love was based on our measuring up. We might also have come to this conclusion when we noticed we were not receiving what we needed from them: "No matter how hard I try, it is never enough for them." That belief was self-negating in childhood, but it is an intriguing irony as we look at it now. It turns out to be true at another level. We do indeed need something more than elbow grease in the pursuit of any significant goal. Something else has to figure in. The Upanishads state: "What is above creation cannot be attained by action." We also see a metaphor in Psalm 127: "Unless the Lord builds the house, they labor in vain who build it." The human psyche, in all traditions, has kept noticing the importance of grace.

The reference to building also reminds us that what begins with determination by some can become grace to others later. For instance, many people have given their lives and put great effort into creating a democracy. We now benefit from their work and sacrifices without having to merit or earn it—though we do need to protect and nurture it.

In religious history, Pelagianism is an example of an overemphasis on effort to the exclusion of the need for grace. Pelagius (fourth century) was a British monk who proposed that our own willpower was enough for salvation. His perspective was condemned in 431 by the First Council of Ephesus, which defended the necessity of grace. In a recent understanding of what Pelagius really meant, we see that his work was not as dualistic as was imagined by the official church. Pelagius viewed reason, understanding, and free will as aspects of grace. Thus, he had an appreciation of the integration of grace and willpower.

This integration happens for any of us when we appreciate grace as intrinsic to every aspect of our true nature. We then do not see grace as an add-on to who we are. We recognize it as a necessary ingredient of our human fulfillment. We notice that sometimes we have access to a special power to believe, feel, know, act, speak, or be that takes us far beyond our usual limitations. Our trust in ourselves is trust in our true nature.

Whenever we have a dualistic notion such as, "I am doing this because I want to achieve a particular state of

consciousness, a particular state of being," then automatically we separate ourselves from the reality of what we are.

—CHÖGYAM TRUNGPA RINPOCHE,
Cutting Through Spiritual Materialism

Not Enough

Too much reliance on effort is one danger, but another is too little trust
in the need for it. Grace loses its meaning when it does not stir and spur
us. We then believe we lead a charmed life instead of being required to
lead a responsible life.

When grace and effort work in an integrated way, we see that grace is
a cue to us to exert ourselves. We can be so pleased with grace, however, that we become overconfident. We imagine that grace will keep
coming our way with no follow-up needed on our part. This is quietism, the belief that we can sit back, rest on our laurels, leave it all to
chance, do nothing but trust that God will provide.

The dictionary defines *quietism* as a passive attitude toward external events, including world politics, a withdrawal from concern about
or participation in public affairs. It is the opposite of activism, excess
focus on effort. The quietist says: "I don't have to do anything." The
activist says: "I have to do everything."

The Greek philosopher Epicurus and the Stoics, including Marcus
Aurelius, had quietist perspectives. The Stoics believed in the ideal of *ap-
atheia*. This apathy is an indifference to events, an absence of reactivity, a
demurring to put effort into making changes. The quietist Stoics believed
that deliverance from anxiety happened as they withdrew themselves
more and more from passion in relationships and participation in politics.

The word *quietism* was used in seventeenth-century Europe to refer
to a form of mysticism. The delight of quietists was to lose themselves
in pure contemplation of God. This absorption in the divine involved
a voluntary annihilation of the self so that the mind and will could become less prominent. Then God would be able to act in the human
soul without hindrance. Effort and spiritual practices were considered
signs of a lack of faith in the divine presence and in graced assistance.

Both Hinduism and Buddhism acknowledge that equanimity is arrived at through letting go of a belief in a separate ego identity and in its power to effect enlightenment.

In Hinduism, the identity of a person resides in the high god Brahma. In Buddhism, liberation from desire and attachment is a release from the sense of a discrete identity, a cause of suffering. In both traditions, nirvana is a snuffing out of the need for activism—and concepts—of any kind. We hear Krishna's advice in the Bhagavad Gita, for instance: "Abandon all supports and look to me for protection" (18:66). "Neither knowledge of the Vedas nor austerity, nor charity, nor sacrifice can bring the vision you have seen" (11:53; Eknath Easwaran translation).

In Buddhism, quietism particularly appears in teachings that recommend meditation as a spiritual path with very little participation in the concerns of society. Engaged Buddhism, however, proposes embracing liberal societal interests as a central part of authentic spiritual practice. Loving-kindness practice is about showing love to all beings, not just aspiring to do so. The authentic path is always a gentle but challenging combination of meditation and action.

Does Merit Matter?

> Without effort or recourse to your mental faculties you can become a Buddha.
>
> —EIHEI DOGEN ZENJI, *Shoji*

Effort is often associated with the gaining of merits. The word *merit* is from the Latin *merēre,* which means "to earn." Merit is defined as something that deserves or justifies a reward, remuneration, or commendation. It is an entitlement to compensation or recognition. Merit in society is acquired by worthy actions, and from it comes our claim to respect, praise, and recompense. Grace is not about the one who is worthy; it is given to all, so it affirms that all of us are worthy.

When we were taught, especially in early life, that we had to earn or merit love, we were taught along with that to lose sight of the element of grace in our lives. Like real love, grace is unconditional; it is not given "on condition that" we have gathered merit.

Grace, also like authentic love, cannot be won. Nor is it based on performance. Most of us are not used to appreciation based on who we are—always and ultimately good. We are more used to appreciation based on how well we have performed, how we have shown goodness. All the years in which it was drilled into our minds that performance and excellence are what matter can obscure our vision of the workings of grace—a gift in us, not based on accomplishment and merit.

It is understandable, however, that we believe our positive actions toward others should prompt them to love us; we trust that our good deeds gain us merit or appeal in their eyes. Yet such beliefs hail from the ego world of entitlements, where we believe that our actions place a claim on others and vice versa.

In true loving-kindness, the world beyond the narrow boundaries of ego, there is no gaining of merits. Mature, spiritually conscious love is not conditioned by anything but existence: "I love you because you are." Shakespeare, in Sonnet 87, alludes to this theme: "The cause of this fair gift in me is wanting." He is saying he has something wonderful in his life that has come to him as a gift. It was not caused by him; that is, it did not happen because of his effort or merit but simply because he exists.

The theological definition of *merit* is "worthiness of spiritual reward acquired by righteous acts." However, the acts themselves are believed to be done under the influence of grace. Since grace cannot be earned, it is thus not the result of merit but the cause of it. This is because human actions can never be salutary enough to merit an eternal reward in heaven. Our actions take on meaning by grace. In other words, our merits are themselves graces. We see this in a teaching of the Council of Trent: "The Lord, whose bounty towards all people is so great, wills that His own gifts be their merits."

Questions arise in theology about merit and grace. If grace is free, how can it be merited? If grace is free, how can there be a reward in heaven? Grace makes heaven a gift, not a reward. Indeed, Saint Augustine wrote: "God crowns your merits, not as your earnings, but as His gifts." He taught that our good works and even our asking for graces happen because of the grace we are given. In his view, and in that of many religious traditions, grace is primary, but spiritual practices and commitments lead to merits nonetheless. The merits do not cause re-wards or graces. They only help place us in a position of openness to grace. The *Catholic Encyclopedia* states: "In the sight of God there is no real merit in the strictest sense of the word."

Merit is also a concept found in some Buddhist teachings. Merit is gained by practices, rituals, meditation, chanting, adherence to pre-cepts, acts of compassion. The three bases by which merit is gained, according to the Khuddaka Nikaya Sutra, are generosity, goodwill, and mental tranquillity. This merit helps move us toward liberation and positively affects both our present life and our future lives.

In some religious traditions merit can be transferred to those who have died. This idea is also found in Buddhism. We read in the Sutra of the Great Vows of Ksitigarbha Bodhisattva that the practitioner can transfer part of his or her own merit to alleviate the suffering or karma that loved ones may be enduring in the afterlife. The Sanskrit word *parinamana* means "dedication" or "transfer of merit," in this instance, something in us that has an effect on others. In Japanese Buddhism, for instance, Ksitigarbha Bodhisattva is called Jizo, the equivalent of a guardian angel. As the bodhisattva of the earth, his merits become pro-tections that are transferred to children and travelers. A bodhisattva is a practitioner who seeks enlightenment not for her own glorification but because she knows it is the best position from which she can help others. For the bodhisattva, inspired by *bodhicitta,* even enlightenment is for and about love.

We notice a consciousness of the ego element of merit and reward in the teachings of Bodhidharma and in the Diamond Sutra. Bodhi-dharma went from China to India in 527 c.e., where he met Emperor Wu, who boasted of his merits based on all he had done to further Bud-dhism in his country. Bodhidharma replied: "There is no such thing as merit in the worldly sense of accomplishment. Merit is pure wisdom, silent and void." The Diamond Sutra also states: "There is no one to give merit, no one to receive merit. There is no merit at all." Likewise in the Zen tradition is the teaching of "no idea of gaining."

At the same time, the fourteenth-century Tibetan Buddhist master Ngulchu Thogme Zangpo offers this dedication of his bodhisattva practices: "May all sentient beings, receiving the merit amassed by the effort I have made in this work, soon reach your attainment, O great Lokesvara, All-Seeing Protector." Here merit is for others' liberation, an example of generosity and loving-kindness.

The idea of individual merit for individual reward is more ego wish than true dharma. Every spiritual practice each of us does is for all beings who are, have been, and will be. Letting go of gaining anything, including merit, is a release from the danger of spiritual materialism, the hoarding of merits we believe will lead to our own liberation. All of our merits, that is, the results of our practices, can only be for the whole human race and all beings with us. That universal love is beyond merit or demerit. It is what a heart looks like when it gives itself utterly to loving-kindness. That heart is the deepest reality of who we are.

> Our way is not to sit to attain something; it is to express our true nature.
> —SHUNRYU SUZUKI, *Zen Mind, Beginner's Mind*

3

Destiny, Fate, and Luck

We are dragged along by fate to the destiny we refuse to walk to upright.

— CARL JUNG, *Answer to Job*

Destiny

Destiny can refer to an irresistible calling or a life purpose. It has to be consciously embraced by us to be fulfilled. This differs from fate, our lot, whether we like it or not. Fate is related to necessity; something has to happen. Destiny, however, may or may not happen. Life can pass us by and time will stand by as we miss the many-splendored thing, fulfillment of our unique purpose on earth.

At some point we realize that we have a destiny, something we are here to do, someone we are here to be. The clues are the gifts and talents we were born with, the sources of bliss that attract us, the sense of a calling.

Our destiny is personal when it is about finding and expressing our authentic identity; loving and being loved; following our deepest needs, values, ideals, and longings.

Our destiny is also collective, a summons to make a contribution to the lives of others and to participate in the evolution of our humanity toward justice, peace, and love. Barbara Marx Hubbard, in *The Evolutionary Journey*, says: "Deep in our consciousness is the need for purpose. We yearn for significance over and beyond our personal goals. It is for relatedness to a higher order that the flame of expectancy burns." In the past, religion was the main vehicle to the fulfillment of that expectancy. Now we find ourselves seeking the architecture of a higher order in a variety of traditions, cultures, and personal experiences.

Sooner or later, all of us notice that the fulfillment of both our personal and collective destiny will take more than the resources we came into the world with, even when joined to those we gain along the way.

Regarding the fulfillment of our personal destiny, we are like carpenters who face the task of building a house. But our toolbox contains only a hammer, pliers, and a wrench. We have the intelligence to know the full set of tools required, and we know we will have to acquire them if we are to complete the job. We have three, a good start. Now we have to buy or borrow the others. To apply this analogy to our topic: We are in the world with intelligence, willpower, and physical stamina. To fulfill our destiny, we will also need inspiration, inventiveness, and creativity. These do not come from us, as did the three tools we brought with us to build the house. They will have to come to us, like the tools we still need. We bring our tools, efforts; we need creative resources, graces. We place ourselves in the best position for this to happen when we cultivate an attitude of receptiveness, humility about our deficits, and gratitude for what we have so far.

Regarding our collective destiny, we are like plasterers being asked to build a new and more glorious Taj Mahal. We have minds big enough to understand the project. But we also know that we do not have all it will take to complete it. For instance, we do not have the inspiration to envision it, the drafting and architectural skills to design it, the sculpting and masonry skills to construct it, the goldsmithing artistry to gold leaf it. We do, however, have superior plastering skills, and if we can work with the other skilled laborers, we can certainly contribute to the completion of the project. To apply this analogy to our topic: We have plastering skills and a willingness to cooperate. Now we need cooperation from the other workers, blueprints of the plan, and direction as to where to do our work. These do not come from us, like our efforts, but come to us, like graces. We place ourselves in the best position for this to happen when we show willingness to collaborate with the other artists and workers. This is a metaphor for how we bring our efforts to align with graces in the collective enterprise of building a just, peaceful, and loving world—a worthy destiny indeed.

In both instances, personal and collective, we have something to offer, and we need something else, though there is no guarantee that what we need will be available to us. What we have is our willpower, our willingness to work, and our openness to receive help. When grace does come through, it may be just enough, or it may exceed what we hoped for.

We came into the world with minds that have less than is needed for the fulfillment of our destiny, but we are graced by a limitless psyche in a limitless universe. Thus, any experience, feeling, thought, event, person, place, or thing can be a channel or form of grace. Grace comes through to us also in nature, dreams, spiritual realizations, intuitions. Each gives us information, a message, a pointer to what comes next on our path. They are all surprising but welcome couriers from the world of grace, the only world over which ego holds no sway and has no say.

Sometimes special people come along who show us what a human destiny can open into. Buddha or Christ can be exemplars, forerunners in the epic of evolution, pioneers in the adventure of being human, scouts who discovered territories in the psyche no one guessed were there. We learn more from models than we do from teachings in lectures or books. Their example offers portraits of what life can be at its best. Letting that flourish in us is how grace works through models in our spiritual development and how transformation of our attitudes and behavior occurs.

Willpower and brawn do not convey us to our destiny. They only help once we have been led across the threshold by powers that surpass our own. We see this in heroic-journey sagas again and again. Grace and effort have to synthesize if a whole story is to be played out. Every hero tale includes this combination of ingredients—our courageous actions and assisting graces—so it must be a reliable description of what the fulfillment of our own destiny requires.

Fate

The fates, Moirai in ancient Greek, Parcae in Latin, ordained each person's destiny. Not even the gods could escape their governance. Plato, in *The Republic,* says that the Fates are the daughters of Ananke, necessity. There is no avoiding them or canceling their plan for us. Aeschylus, in *Prometheus Bound,* sums it up: "Fate [Moirai] brings everything to its fulfillment.... Our skill is much weaker than Necessity [Ananke]. Indeed, not even Zeus can escape what is fated." Thus, fate has a style in common with grace, since both override the role of effort. But unlike grace, fate most often refers to tragic, irredeemable outcomes. This is called cosmic irony, all of us at the mercy of a cruel fate. For example, in Shakespeare's *Macbeth,* Macduff says this when he finds out about the deaths of his innocent wife and children: "Did heaven look on and not take their part?" Macduff imputes helplessness even to the gods over the power of inexorable fate.

The Fates were personified as three sisters who operate sequentially in terms of human life. Clotho, Greek for "spinner," spins the thread of human life from distaff to spindle. Her Latin name was Nona, "Ninth," because women prayed to her in the final month of pregnancy for a healthy life and good fortune for the infant about to be born.

Lachesis, Greek for "one who allots," measures the thread of our life. She decides how long we will live. Her Latin name was Decima, "Tenth," since her work comes after that of her sister Clotho.

Atropos, Greek for "inevitable," cuts the thread at our death in accord with the lifeline Lachesis has allotted us. She also chooses the kind of death we will have. Her Latin name is Morta, "Death."

In *The Republic* we hear the three sisters singing the tunes of the Sirens who lure sailors to their death, as described in Homer's *Odyssey.* Clotho sings of what is; Lachesis sings of what has been; Atropos sings of what will be. Thus, for Plato, the Fates preside over our story from beginning to end. Plato is suggesting that happenings in the past, present, and future have an element of inevitability, necessity. The Fates can dangerously obsess us, luring us to destruction, as in the metaphor of the Sirens. What happens is beyond our control, yet we are drawn to it, like lovesick sailors drawn by Sirens' songs to an unguessed but definite doom.

The Roman goddess of fate was Fortuna. She was revered under this title in medieval times as the one who spins the Wheel of Fortune. Fortuna was pictured as blindfolded to show her erratic nature. The blindfold also shows that her dispensing of fortune, good or ill, is arbitrary, not based on merit.

Boethius, in his *Consolation of Philosophy*, wrote of her: "No one can ever be truly secure until he has been forsaken by Fortuna." This makes sense because only when we are abandoned by fortune do we learn to trust ourselves. His statement also aligns with his reporting of this comment by Fortuna: "Inconstancy is my very essence; it is the game I never cease to play as I turn my wheel in its ever changing circle, filled with joy as I bring the top to the bottom and the bottom to the top. Yes, rise up on my wheel if you like, but don't count it an injury when, by the same token, you begin to fall, as the rules of the game will require."

The Wheel of Fortune is depicted in the Tarot deck. It was also used in medieval architecture as the rose window of a cathedral. The medieval wheel was often pictured as having four sections representing the stages of life. Each side showed a human figure who is "reigning," what to us might now be called controlling. The one on the left says, in effect: "I will be in control." The one on top says: "I am in control." The one on the right says: "I have been in control." The one on the bottom says: "I am not in control anymore." (What a sobering summary of our human story.) It is important to notice that the four sections are not equally divided. They are not equal quadrants, since it is Lady Fortune who decides how long each phase will last for each of us. So maintaining control remains out of our hands in any case. What a way to nullify ego entitlement.

In adult spiritual consciousness there is no fate in the sense of fatalism, as in a superstitious belief in predetermined events or outcomes.

There are only the consequences of deliberate choices, and it is up to us to face them. There are givens in life, predicaments that happen to us. It is up to us to handle them. But there is no inevitable twist to our story that has to occur no matter what we do. A belief in that sort of fatalism—what might also be referred to as kismet—can be a shirking of responsibility, a denial of how the world works, a refuge in victimhood, fueled by fear.

Grace is the antidote to the fear of fate. This is because grace is the spiritual advantage that can be found in any event. No matter how desperate our predicament, there is an opportunity for growth in it. Once we trust in grace, we're able to reject any fate as final or binding. We realize that things can happen beyond our control, but there is nothing that *has* to happen and over which we have no possibility of control.

There is always a door, with the grace provided to walk on and through it. Grace in this context was described by Joseph Campbell in his interview with Bill Moyers: "When you are no longer compelled by desire or fear . . . , when you have seen the radiance of eternity in all the forms of time . . . , when you follow your bliss . . . , doors will open where you would not have thought there were doors . . . , and the world steps in and helps."

Finally, we notice that in Buddhism there is a wheel of cyclic existence. It is also referred to as the wheel of becoming, *bhavacakra.* It is a symbolic depiction of the Buddhist path, open to all, and turning on its own, no matter what we do or how we practice.

The Wheel of Dharma, the *dharmacakra,* was one of the symbolic emblems of rulers in ancient India. The concept was that a great wheel would be needed for the chariot that could traverse their far-spread empire. Buddhists used that same symbol to refer to how the Buddha, the king of dharma, can swiftly spread his truth throughout the entire world.

Buddha's enlightenment is indeed always manifesting itself; it has no off switch. Not only is it on continuously, but it manifests itself exactly in the ways each of us can grasp. Every moment is thus a synchronicity of an external circumstance and an interior opportunity to awaken. This limitless quality of dharma is how grace is always within reach for us as individuals and how it endures as the basis of our optimism about the possibility of an enlightened humanity.

Luck

Fate is related to chance in that we can't control it. Chance is random, that is, without a direction, goal, purpose, or apparent logic.

Luck is meaningful chance that leads to a material or ego-advancing gain. Luck helps us *get* more.

Grace is meaningful chance that contributes to the shaping of our destiny. Grace helps us *be* more.

Both luck and grace offer opportunity. We are given an opportunity with luck to use our material gain for good or ill. We are given an opportunity with grace to expand who we are in the present and to advance in what we can become. The opportunity in grace is our cue to engage in practices that help us toward psychological and spiritual growth. Our psychological growth leads to our personal fulfillment; our spiritual advancement includes a sense of our commitment to the human collective.

Both luck and grace offer an advantage. We are given a bonus in the ego world, an edge, a leg up in the pursuit of our ambitions. In the world of the higher self, our true nature, grace enriches our spiritual awareness.

The ego believes that it deserves luck and doesn't need grace. The higher self knows that grace is everywhere and we always need it.

Luck and grace have these qualities in common:

- There is no cause/effect relationship.
- They are beyond our control.
- They cannot be willed into existence.
- Their course cannot be predicted.
- They are improbable but not impossible.
- An advantage to us is always possible.

Luck reminds us of the distinction between chance and choice. We notice three possible circumstances in life: Sometimes there is both choice and chance; sometimes there is only chance; sometimes there is only choice. We see examples of these in three favorite games:

Poker combines chance and choice: The hand we are dealt is based on chance, but skill in playing our cards is in our hands. The enjoyment of the game is in the combination of chance and choice.

In dice, the thrill is in being at the mercy of chance. No skill is required or possible. The odds are even, as in tossing a coin. This is pure chance.

In chess, the enjoyment is entirely skill. Chance does not figure in. There are no random elements, no variables. Winning depends on our level of skill and the lack of equal skill in our partner.

After Luck, What?

Tyche, Greek for "chance" or "luck," was the goddess who presided over the fortune and prosperity of city-states. She is the Greek equivalent of the Roman goddess Fortuna.

Tyche was unpredictable, arbitrary, capricious in her distribution of good or bad luck. All people could hope for was that Tyche *might* be kind to them as individuals in specific instances. Sacrifices at her temples were thought to please her, while yet not guaranteeing a favorable response from her. As we saw above, effort does not guarantee grace. We also see here the belief that still resides in the human psyche: Petitionary prayer and rituals can evoke graces. For instance, we hear this about the goddess ritual at ancient Eleusis in Homer's *Hymn to Demeter:* "Graced is he who has participated in these mysteries."

If Tyche did grace someone with good fortune, three responses were required from the recipient. Those who did not observe these three practices might meet up with Nemesis, the goddess of retribution. She appears in Greek tragedies as the one who strikes those who show hubris. She was also referred to as Adrasteia, "the inescapable."

The three required responses to grace or luck were as follows:

1. No boasting about it or about how you deserved it—a way of avoiding hubris and acknowledging that the gift was from a source beyond ego
2. Offering a sacrifice in thanksgiving—a way of showing gratitude by giving in return
3. Showing generosity to the poor—a way of acknowledging that gifts are meant to be shared and that grace is a moving experience that wants to keep moving through us to others

These three ancient responses to grace ingeniously point us to useful responses to grace in our lives today:

In the first, no boasting about how you deserved it, we see a warning against naive individualism. Grace, in the ego's interpretation, is about "me" as special: "My receiving this grace is a sign that I am privileged." Since grace is not based on merit, it is not privilege but gift, not wages but bonus. This recognition leads us to appreciate what we receive rather than believe ourselves entitled, an important way to let go of ego.

Second, we are enjoined to show gratitude. This is not: "I am thankful for this special favor to me." That might further inflate one's ego: "I have an in with the powers so I get a special deal." Gratitude is an antidote to such entitlement. It is a response to a largesse that transcends any one-to-one focus. We are thankful to be part of humanity and to be continually sharing in gifts from sources that seem to care about us.

Third, to receive a grace is to take on the responsibility of sharing what we received with others. This is yet another way of acknowledging that grace is not about "me only" but is always about all of us. We consider someone who has talent and keeps it to her- or himself as selfish because we realize intuitively that all talents are meant to be shared. Grace evokes our effort to engage in sharing what we have received. This fits with how grace is a mobile reality that moves through us to everyone.

Synchronously, while writing this section, I read Michael Lewis's commencement address to the class of 2012 at Princeton: "Life's outcomes, while not entirely random, have a huge amount of luck baked into them. Above all, recognize that if you have had success, you have also had luck. And with luck comes obligation. You owe a debt, and not just to your gods. You owe a debt to the unlucky." This helps us see the link between receiving and sharing with compassion.

In mature spiritual consciousness, grace from a higher power—deeply interior power—is not simply a lucky break. It is an unconditional acceptance of us, nothing left out, nothing rejected or deemed unworthy of us within the family of humanity. When we feel this action of grace at work in us, we come to accept ourselves and others too. This is because grace unifies us; it cuts through our illusion of separation. Fate blesses some and curses others. Luck divides the lucky from the unlucky. Grace is a new regime of connectedness where we are finally awakened from the trance of separateness.

> Grace is more than gifts. In grace something is overcome; grace occurs in spite of something; grace occurs in spite of separation and estrangement. Grace is the reunion of life with life, the reconciliation of the self with itself. Grace is the acceptance of that which is rejected.
>
> —PAUL TILLICH, *The Shaking of the Foundations*

4

The Gift of Synchronicity

There is a bridge connecting time and eternity. This bridge
is the spirit in every human person.

—UPANISHADS

As we look at our life, it feels like a story—coherent and with a
progressing plotline. It has a trajectory with a beginning, a middle, and someday an end. It seems to fall into chapters and themes.
There are characters coming and going. Some enter the yarn by chance
and then become highly significant. Some seem significant at first but
then fade in importance. Some further the predictable plot; some inter-
rupt it so that it takes an entirely new direction. It is a short step to
wondering if there is some hand at work in all the mysterious coincidences and choices. We have no way of knowing for sure, but sometimes we feel an abiding presence in our story. That presence is not a
noun but a verb: ever-moving grace, showing itself in all the synchronicities that happen to us.

In his essay "Synchronicity: An Acausal Connecting Principle,"
Carl Jung describes synchronicity as "a meaningful coincidence of two
or more events, in which something other than the probability of
chance is involved." The "something other" is a power that transcends
human or chance interventions.

A coincidence is not synchronicity when it is the result of mere chance. Synchronicity is meaningful chance. Random or mere chance is simply accidental and without coincidental significance. For instance, if your name, reader, is David, like mine, that is indeed a coincidence but not synchronicity, since it does not have any significance in either of our lives. Our names' being the same does not mean that something momentous will happen, that our psyches will be transformed, that we will discover an as yet unknown purpose in our life, that we will suddenly open hitherto locked gates in our psyche or soul, that we will fulfill our singular destinies—some of the ways events become meaningful. The name David that was given to me and you is only an accidental similarity, not a meaningful one. Of course, if this paragraph or our identical names were to lead to a whole new chapter for either of us, then a synchronous meaning *is* on tap.

Synchronistic events are ultimately meaningful in the sense that they guide us or confirm us on our path. They are also meaningful in that they can

- reveal our authentic needs, values, longings, and wishes;
- release our true feelings;
- show us our unique calling;
- connect us to others—including a partner—and the world, since synchronicity is an indicator of relatedness.

Often we are not aware of the meaning of a synchronous event in this parade of days until a long time after it has occurred. What we might think of as totally our own accomplishment turns out to have had a hidden grace factor. What we might imagine to be mere coincidence turns out to represent a larger purpose at work than our ego can contain or explain. Thus, synchronicity gives us a clue to the deep underlay of purpose and meaning in the universe and how they are revealing themselves in our lives. We then might come to suspect the presence of invisible alliances that are helping us. They feel both beyond and within us—like the transcendent, like grace, like love.

Indeed, psyche and universe are not two discrete realities. Carl Jung also proposes, in "Synchronicity: An Acausal Connecting Principle," that synchronicity shows us that our psyche is not limited to our cranium: "Synchronicity designates . . . chance happenings . . . so improbable that we must assume that they are based on some kind of principle. . . . From this it follows that either the psyche cannot be localized in space or that space is relative to the psyche." Thus psyche extends into the universe. Synchronicity helps us acknowledge the unity of psyche and matter—ourselves and all that is. We see the extent, or rather boundlessness, of psychic life in an experience of synchronicity, the mirror relationship between mind and matter. We see that we are not alone. We are held in a grander orbit than we ever guessed by the size of ourselves or even of the planet.

The English poet George Herbert saw this transcendent holding of us as a sign of our being loved by a transcendent power: "O mighty love! Man is one world, and hath another to attend him." Synchronicity in this view is grace as a power that embraces and enfolds us.

This does not mean that we have a safe conduct through life. All we have is what a lover has in the arms of the beloved—a sense of accompaniment when we are quaking but not protection from an earthquake about to happen. The theologian Paul Tillich, speaking of providence in *The Shaking of the Foundations,* expressed this well: "Providence does not mean a divine planning by which everything is predetermined. . . . Providence means that there is a creative and saving possibility implied in every situation, which cannot be destroyed by any event. Providence means that the demonic and destructive forces within ourselves and our world can never have an unbreakable grasp upon us, and that the bond which connects us with fulfilling love can never be disrupted."

We will thus be able to find opportunities for spiritual practice and spiritual progress in any perilous circumstance. With that option always available, and our yes to it, all that happens becomes a meaningful coincidence: just exactly what happens is exactly what can help us grow.

Carl Jung also wrote in his foreword to *The I Ching:* "Synchronicity takes the events in space and time as meaning more than mere chance." Something unknown is doing we don't know what or why, yet a meaning comes through to us.

Synchronicity is a vehicle by which assisting forces come our way on our way but not because of our ways. Meaningful coincidences are beyond our planning or control. As such they can be powerful and convincing indicators that more is afoot in our world than what we do or are in control of.

Grace has three elements: it is a benefit, it is not based on effort, and it is from a transcendent source. Likewise, synchronous events that show us our path are beneficial. We can't make them happen, so they are beyond effort. They come from a source beyond our ego. This is how an experience of synchronicity is a grace. At the same time, synchronicity is also a wonderfully clear demonstration of how grace shows itself.

Synchronicity appears in many forms. Here are some of the most common:

- A coincidence of or striking similarity between two events or experiences
- A fortuitous event or occasion that makes a difference in how our life proceeds
- An accident or disability that leads to a creative path for us
- A trigger to a chain of events that leads to a new direction in our life
- A psychic perception and a simultaneously happening event (as in extrasensory perception)
- A series of events that show us a path, for example, losses that lead us to let go, opportunities that lead us to take hold
- A symptom that is a pointer to where we need self-healing
- A meeting of two people who did not plan to meet but who will embark on an important relationship
- Words or actions that prove true in a larger sense than intended: "Little did I know then how prophetic her words were"

- An image that is fascinating to us and endures over the years, which gradually reveals something significant about our destiny
- Rituals that are outward signs of a corresponding interior grace
- A resemblance between a dream and an event that follows, as if predicted
- Dreams that show us what is really happening in ourselves and others or point to new possibilities or dangers to watch out for
- Divination and astrology revealing our patterns and the possibilities in our future

These are all examples of grace at work because they provide opportunities for personal fulfillment and spiritual growth. They show us how events can be friendly, so we don't have to fear or run from what happens. We can trust that it leads us into the depths of who we are and what the world wants of us.

Here is one final example of what synchronicity might look like:

A friend whose husband had died told me she was having visions of him, that he was definitely communicating with her sometimes. I asked about the visions and realized she was receiving important information about the meaning of the relationship and of the path opening to her now. She wondered if she were possessed or going insane. Suddenly, she asked me point blank: "Do you think these are hallucinations or actual visits?" I said: "I see them as graces."

I see my friend's experience as an instance of a meaningful coincidence between life's questions and love's reply, irrepressible even in death. When we have an experience like the one my friend described, we don't walk away from it. We enter it, pay attention to it. Then the grace dimension comes through to us. We lose interest in explanations that have to align with logic or with what the Board of Psychiatry deems normal. (After all, normal is not necessarily the same as healthy—or ecstatic.)

Trusting Opportunities

> [We are] accepting our actual companions and circum-
> stances, however humble or odious, as the mystic officials
> to whom the universe has delegated its whole pleasure
> for us.
>
> —RALPH WALDO EMERSON, "ESSAY ON EXPERIENCE"

The main challenge that synchronicity presents to us is the imperative to pronounce, over and over, an unconditional yes to what happens to us. We see how this means not losing sight of the graces in the wide net of life's events and relationships. With a yes to what is, we can walk more easily through any predicament, not necessarily unscathed but able to find ways of renewing ourselves in the process. This happens because of the synchronicity between the opportunities we are offered and our recognition of their value. Then our life events and relationships show us what we need to know or how to grow, what makes a coincidence meaningful, what reveals the presence of grace.

Synchronicity also shows us where what we are choosing may be out of alignment with what needs to happen for us to evolve. We may notice, in a series of pointed coincidences or dreams, some inner rhythms and inclinations that may not match the decisions we are making. We see that the conventional milestones of life may not be appropriate for our unique path in this particular moment. We might resonate with something Virginia Woolf wrote in her notebook: "There are waves by which a life is marked, a rounding off that has nothing to do with events." Synchronicities show us the real waves and invite us into them.

We can recognize the invitation in synchronicity as the *spur* of the moment. That word *spur* is a fitting metaphor; synchronicity can move us but can also hurt at times, as in the hard knocks that are ultimately growing pains. For instance, a terrible accident can lead to a long recovery during which we redesign our life in a way that releases hitherto pent-up creativity or spirituality. A negative event like that can become the synchronous spur that leads to a positive outcome. To trust synchronicity in our lives is to welcome the spur it provides; however, we do well to remember that a spur can also cut.

To be open to synchronicity is a sign of spiritual progress, a sign that we are trusting an assisting power in the universe. We are aware that our life is happening in a vaster terrain than can be measured by our home address. We are acknowledging that our consciousness is not limited to our brain or mind but extends into the immeasurable reaches of the universe.

We know that we are trusting synchronicity as a force that helps us know ourselves and our journey when we

- acknowledge grace in our daily life and in the story of our life so far and are grateful;
- take all that happens to us, for good or ill, as opportunities for our psychological growth and spiritual progress;
- honor a coherent series of coincidences as worthy of our attention about what may be next for us;
- believe that we are here on the planet at precisely this time to fulfill our life purpose of cocreating a world of justice, peace, and love, and we trust that graces will come to us to outfit us for this challenge;
- cherish and use the gifts we were born with as revelations of our calling;
- see how many events and inner longings have helped us know more clearly where our bliss really lies;
- gain clues from what has happened to us about our deepest needs, values, and wishes;
- realize that every relationship we have found ourselves in has provided us occasions for understanding ourselves better and for practicing loving-kindness;
- appreciate the friends who have come along in our lives as supports and models on our journey;
- remain aware of the combination of challenges and comforts that keep arising in all of our connections with people and institutions;

- see that our deficits and deficiencies, including the mistakes we have made in the course of life, are all grist for the mill of creativity and transformation;
- glimpse an emerging design behind all the chaos that has occurred in our lives;
- see how every loss has shown us where to let go and move on;
- see how every opportunity has shown us where to take hold and persevere;
- become aware of how each person, place, thing, and event of our life has been an assisting force on our journey;
- notice that our life experiences have coincided with our growing commitment to a love that can be unconditional, a wisdom that is unfailing, and a lively force of healing for ourselves and others;
- see how everything has moved us in three directions: we are finding the serenity to accept what cannot be changed, growing in the courage to change what can be changed, gaining the wisdom to know the difference;
- recognize how the givens of life are truly the ingredients for our growth in character, depth, and compassion as we continue to say yes to them and remain open to what may come next—the appropriate style of people on a journey;
- continually turn to nature as a powerful resource and see that our life is mirrored in its seasons, births, deaths, and renewals;
- are thankful for each of the meaningful coincidences that make up this list and are saying yes courageously to what may come next.

Each entry on the list refers to an ideal of psychological and spiritual progress most of us have not yet reached. Yet each item on the list can serve as an aspiration. An aspiration is an intention to open to grace; it can also be a prayer. For instance, we can restate the sentence "We glimpse an emerging design behind all the chaos that has occurred in our lives" as an aspiration: "May I keep glimpsing an emerging design behind any chaos that has occurred in my life."

Synchronicity is not objective and provable. It is known by feeling and experience—not scientific criteria. We might have a hard time convincing others of the synchronicities in our lives. We recall that the heroic-journey story ends with the heroine describing the wonders she has seen. But the words often fall on deaf ears. Only those who have experienced grace will believe in it. Then all the heroine can do is appreciate her own experience and hope that others find what she found.

The last scene of the film *The Wizard of Oz* shows Dorothy waking up in her own bed back in Kansas. The three friends, the wizard, her aunt and uncle are around her. When Dorothy tells of her adventure, her aunt says: "You just had a bad dream." Dorothy replies: "It wasn't a dream; it was a place," and pointing to the three farmhands and the wizard, she adds: "and you and you and you and you were there." They all look at her with gentle kindness but with obvious disbelief, and she exclaims: "Doesn't anybody believe me?" We are reminded of Joseph Campbell's description of the returning hero who "has to confront . . . good people at a loss to comprehend."

Finally, realizing that her experience is her own and that others can't be convinced of its authenticity, Dorothy does what any enlightened person would do. She drops the topic and rests in mindful awareness of the here and now: "But anyway, Toto, we're home, home, and this is my room and you're all here and I love you all."

Choice and Chance

Grace will always remain a mystery to us. Certitude about it is contrary to respect for such an enigma. Only openness to and gratitude for its arrival are appropriate. What arrives is the something, we know not what, that accompanies, assists, and allies with us, we know not how. But we do know that this graced something is not from our familiar ego. Though it is mysterious, we glimpse the source of grace in three ways: our sense of a higher power, our contact with own true nature, and our touching into the life force of the universe. In deep spiritual consciousness, we come to realize that all three of these are one single seamless reality.

In such consoling awareness, there is a danger: we might exaggerate the role of grace in our lives. An important feature of adulthood is acknowledging our choices as our own. Grace does not supplant, cancel, or coerce human choice, but only offers it support, healing, elevation. We are always free to say no; we remain free when we say yes. Grace and freedom are meant to work together; they are cooperative, not oppositional. Grace prompts, but it does not poke. Grace does not make something happen; it opens the door, and it will always be up to us to walk through it. And, yes, sometimes the ability or courage it may take to walk through is itself a grace.

Just as we can't legitimately say, "The devil made me do it," we can't accurately say, "I know I made the right choice because I was following the lead of synchronicity, grace, or inspiration from a divine voice." This sense of certainty about what can't be certain downgrades or cancels the sense of mystery. We bargain away some of our own accountability for the choices we make. Then we can't be self-determined and responsible—what helps us develop psychologically.

Our most accurate declaration is, "I am thankful for whatever assistance was with me, but nonetheless, it was I who made the choice." Later, if regrets arise, we have nowhere, material or spiritual, to place blame. Our saving practice is always a yes to the given that some human decisions will prove unskillful, no matter how smart we are, but every decision eventually offers an opportunity for growth, no matter who we are.

We are all on the seesaw of personal choice and meaningful chance. We continue to wonder how much of what happens in our lives is a consequence of our choices and how much is the result of spiritual forces that resist our grasp. There will never be a definitive answer to this question. We will always wonder—wonder being one of our best graces indeed. A state of wonder is not so bad a place to be when we are on a journey.

Synchronicity as the archetype of grace is a common motif in history and in stories. In the central story of our humanity, the heroic journey, we notice that multiple coincidences occur. They point the hero or heroine to his or her destiny or present opportunities for wisdom or courage. Here are some examples that span the centuries: In Greek myth Athena gives a wonderful shield to Perseus so he can do battle with Medusa. In Mozart's opera *The Magic Flute,* the queen's ladies give the flute to Tamino to aid him in saving Pamina. In the 1940 film *The Thief of Bagdad,* the thief flies a magic carpet to save his friend Ahmed from execution. In Harper Lee's *To Kill a Mockingbird,* Boo saves Scout and Jem from death by coming to their rescue just in time.

Those synchronous moments and surprising gifts are not caused by the hero but come to him or her as graces. In fact, what makes a man or a woman a hero is precisely that realization. Every exertion was a collaboration between the hero's choices and graced powers beyond his or her grip or power to fathom. But he or she never knows for sure which was which. *How much was I and how much was grace?* The only certainty is the appropriateness of gratitude.

Here is a chart that helps us see how grace and free choice can work together in various chapters of life:

Life Concerns	*Meaningful Chance or Grace: What Happens to Us*	*Our Choice: What We Do with What Happens*
Childhood	We have effective, caring parents who provide a safe and secure atmosphere for our healthy development	We appreciate our parents and make the best of what they offer, not expecting them to be perfect
Relationship	We meet a partner who shows love, is trustworthy, can communicate, is not self-centered but cooperative	We appreciate what the partner offers and we act the same way toward her or him
Health	We have a strong constitution, good genes, a robust immune system	We practice health habits, maintain a good diet, stay fit, do not abuse alcohol or drugs

Life Concerns	Meaningful Chance or Grace: What Happens to Us	Our Choice: What We Do with What Happens
Career	We have a talent or interest at the right place at the right time for an opportunity to practice it	We have, use, and increase the skills needed to advance creatively in our work
Creativity	We are born with certain talents and are given opportunities to find out what they are and use them; we are inspired with an artistic vision	We practice our art or endeavor to increase our natural capacities and put them to use in ways that reflect our own uniqueness
Spirituality	We are introduced to the spiritual dimension in life or we experience a personal awakening that opens us to it	We engage in spiritual practices that help us explore and discover ever-new possibilities

When Synchronicity Comes as Inspiration

Synchronicity as the archetype of assistance can come to us in the form of intuitions that fit the needs of the moment or inspirations that advance our creative impulse.

Carl Jung reported an experience of a *spiritus rector*—a guiding spirit operating mostly unconsciously. This is a way of referring to grace, a power that assists us but can't be summoned or extinguished. We can say no to using this gift, but we can't stop it from being offered.

This can also be seen in how, though we can use our creative skills, inspiration seems to be out of our hands. This may be why inspiration is often personified as a muse—a figure beyond our control—another way of referring to an arbitrary power we may receive but cannot conjure. Emily Dickinson acknowledged the muse, a personification of grace, when she wrote of "hands I cannot see" with regard to messages that came to her from nature and found their way into her poems.

We feel creative inspiration or energy as coming *through* us rather than *from* us. Imagination is an organ of grace since it opens and expands our creativity. As with any grace, we realize the importance of following up with disciplined effort. For instance, we have a talent for poetry or music. That innate aptitude, ours without effort, is a grace. But it is then up to us to write out the poem or song, channeling that grace, using the skills we have learned. That is the effort, our part of the bargain. We are reminded of what the Venerable Bede said in the eighth century about Caedmon, the monk considered to be the first English poet: "There was in that monastery a brother upon whom *heaven had bestowed the gift* of writing verses." (Emphasis is mine.)

Mozart reported that he "heard" a piece in his head as a complete unity before writing it. Then it was up to him to do the musical notation. This is an example of the interplay of grace and effort, gift and use of the gift, a cooperative venture between work and aptitude/gift. Grace comes by meaningful chance; our response is meaningful choice.

The muse is associated with inspiring the artist. But the gift of the muse also comes through when we readers, listeners, and viewers are affected by art. The muse touches Mozart but also touches us when we hear his work. When we say a concerto moves us, we are acknowledging a feature of grace, since we are not moving ourselves but being moved by a force beyond our ego and will. There is thus a gift dimension in both the aesthetic creation of the artist and the responses of appreciation by the public. This also reminds us that nothing of value is complete when it stands alone; its fulfillment is in its being shared. In this sense art is another form of giving and receiving, a spiritual enterprise.

In ancient times creativity was considered a divine gift. Creative, artistic people were thought to have what in Greek was called a *daimon*, in Latin a *genius*. This was an invisible force that instilled inspiration and creative power in the artist. Art was thought to come through the artist, not from him or her, and it was meant for the surrounding world. Daimons and geniuses were assisting forces that hovered over the artist. This meant that his or her success was owing to a power higher than the ingenuity of ego could construct. It is easy to see this as another description of grace. It also, of course, accounts for the capriciousness of inspiration.

Since Renaissance times and into our own day, most of us no longer acknowledge that we have geniuses who help us; we are the geniuses. What an example of how our sense of grace as a factor of human experience and accomplishment has diminished. To recover appreciation of transcendent help would be to feel our own humility and our sense of mysterious companionship, two resplendent graces indeed.

Calling and Coincidence

> Grace rises up out of the very substance of one's life, making the riddle to be: "What will become of me if I were to surrender completely to this grace? What will become of me if I do not?"
>
> —JAMES FINLEY, *The Contemplative Heart*

A calling can be felt as an inclination toward or passion for a career, a mission, a vocation. We are moved to pursue a way of life that seems to fit our talents and that certainly endows us with bliss. This sense of calling manifests as an inner conviction or purpose that can't be silenced or evaded.

We may lack the confidence to believe we have talents. Sometimes it takes the insight of others to see gifts in us that we have not yet noticed. A good motto then might be "I step up to the plate on which others see me." This is how we welcome our gifts, find our calling, trust ourselves more. All that remains for us to do is expend the effort to advance our skill level. Then our actions catch up with our gifts.

Since a calling is not earned, benefits us and others, and comes from beyond ourselves, it is a grace. With a calling come graces tailored to support it. These follow-up graces are examples of synchronicity—a coincidence between our calling and being endowed with the special gifts that help us fulfill it. For instance, if we were born with a strong and natural ability to be teachers, we can usually trust that exactly the graces that fit that calling will be in us: studying, planning, ease in front of a group, ability to explain concepts, patience with the learning curve in the variety of students in a class.

In fact, we can sometimes know our calling by the graces that come to us. For instance, if we notice a natural wisdom and know-how in our interactions with children, that may be a sign that we have found our calling to work with children or to be parents.

Sometimes graces are asynchronous. They do not quite match our calling. For instance, I myself am an introvert, and that fits my writing orientation but does not fit marketing myself, now an important part of success in writing. In addition, I seem to hold the archetype of teacher. Yet, as an introvert, I still feel a mild shyness standing before a class. I am not nervous or diffident, but I do notice it is hard for me to keep eye contact with my audience. I teach because I feel it is my calling, not because I am fully cut out for it; that is, I don't have the fully uninhibited rapport with an audience that comes naturally to an extrovert.

However, both in writing and in teaching, I was given the gift of explaining difficult concepts in ways people can understand, and I believe I can sometimes express myself in a way that moves others. I did not make any of this happen; these are innate gifts for which I am thankful. All I added was practice, and I want to continue to do that with great alacrity.

The disparity that can occur between the grace of talent and the supportive graces that go with it is not a joke on us by the universe. It is an indication of our interconnectedness. Incomplete grace shows how much we need others. We are reminded of what Lucretius says in *On the Nature of Things:* "In order to survive, all mortal beings need one another . . . passing on life's torch, like relay runners in a race."

By meaningful coincidence we seem to meet those we need, and those who need us seem to find us too. Our deficiencies are our matchmakers. We are continually compelled to seek those who can compensate for what we lack. I do this in my writing projects when I cooperate with the marketing department of my publisher. In my teaching career, I say yes often to offers to teach. I am overcoming any obstacles owing to my introversion by continual willingness to put myself out there. I notice I look at people in my audience more now than I did twenty years ago—but still not fully.

There is another area in which graces do not mesh with human choices. Grace sometimes seems forced on the recipient. Jonah refused his calling, the grace to share religious teachings with Assyrian gentiles. A whale swallowed him and, after three days and nights, spit him out once he was finally willing to teach the people of Nineveh. Archetypal stories portray how grace is at times discomfiting and unwelcome but is successful in moving us. Jonah could not evade his destiny. It may also happen, however, that we refuse a grace or calling and no power intervenes to set us on track.

As an aside, Jonah's apparent gift for oratory reminds us that gifts can be used for good or ill. Some people use their gifts to make a contribution to humanity; others use them to cause harm and mayhem. Both Martin Luther King Jr. and Adolph Hitler had the gift of oratory. One helped the world; the other damaged it.

We may admire revolutionary souls whose calling is truly demanding. We may regret or feel ashamed that we do not put ourselves out there more often in courageous, risky ways, especially in speaking up against evil and injustice. But self-sacrifice is a heroic calling indeed. Here is an example. Franz Jägerstätter (1907–1943), a Catholic farmer in Austria, refused to participate in the Nazi war machine. While in prison in Berlin, a bishop and several priests pleaded with him to give up his conscientious objections. They explained that he could find a way to serve the fatherland without guilt, especially if this meant saving his own life and thereby not abandoning his wife and children. According to the bishop, Franz responded: "I'm sorry, Your Reverence, but you just haven't been given this grace that came to me and that I have to honor." Franz was executed by guillotine at age thirty-six. His sentence was officially nullified in Berlin in 1997. He was beatified by Pope Benedict XVI in 2007, the last step toward sainthood.

The grace to die for a cause, given to saintly people like Franz Jägerstätter and Joan of Arc, is not given to everyone. Not everyone wants it, nor would it make sense for society to have it that way. In each generation the world needs all varieties of human callings. Each of us has his or her own. Each of us can respect that of others. It is not that we are cowards when we are not willing to be activists. We all make our contribution to a better world by what we can offer. If we are not political activists but appreciate their commitment, we can acknowledge them with gratitude and offer daily aspirations or prayers for their success: "May those called to activism be safe, courageous, and loving." This is how any of us can be an assisting force in maintaining the human spirit of heroism.

The saints and great heroes were just as messed up as we sometimes are but they did not let that stop them from practicing loving-kindness. What makes them saints is that they did not let their limitations get in the way of their calling. They stepped up to the plate with all their fears and neuroses. They are models for us not because they were perfect but because they did not give up on their capacity to love—or on anyone else's.

Finally, we do keep noticing that graces are offered to us to advance our unique development. When we deny or refuse a grace, we limit our blooming into the tree we can be. Every event in life offers an opportunity to awaken to our destiny or to avoid it. We all have regrets as we look back over our lives and realize that an opportunity, a grace, had come to us and we said no to it. We look back now and realize that our fear or misjudgment held us back from advancing in wisdom or showing more love. When we experience regrets and self-recriminations, we might adopt an affirmation like this: "I use this regret as a cue and a spur to engage in my spiritual practices; I make amends for what I have done or failed to do, if necessary and appropriate. I show more loving-kindness to myself and everyone. I am thankful for all the ways my regrets can turn from curses to graces."

> Everything without exception is an instrument and means of sanctification, provided that the present moment is all that matters.
>
> —JEAN PIERRE DE CAUSSADE, S.J.

5

Grace in the Feminine

It is you alone, goddess, who oversees the nature of all that
is. Without you nothing arises onto the shores of light. . . .
Be my guide in writing this poem about the way things are.
　　　　　　　　　　—LUCRETIUS, *On the Nature of Things*

When you give yourself, give completely, without demand,
without condition, without reservation so that all in you
shall belong to the Divine Mother and nothing left to the
ego or given to any other power. The more complete your
faith, sincerity, and surrender, the more will grace and protection be with you.
　　　　　　—SRI AUROBINDO, *The Mother*, "DIVINE GRACE
　　　　　　　AND FAITH, SINCERITY, AND SURRENDER"

Giving birth as a feminine activity is both real and a metaphor for
transformation, a spiritual birth that brings to life an identity beyond ego. Thus, in Apuleius's *The Golden Ass*, an ancient Latin novel
about a proud lawyer who is transformed by the divine feminine, we
read: "The initiation ceremony [into the feminine mysteries of Isis]
took the form of a kind of voluntary death [of ego], and salvation

through divine grace." In ancient times, it was believed that birth into a new life happens through the divine feminine powers of grace.

Traditions are unanimous in identifying grace as feminine. In myth the Great Mother of the cosmos is honored as the source of grace. Likewise, we associate the natural world with the feminine, hence we use the term *Mother Nature*. We also speak of Lady Luck when referring to outcomes over which the logical mind has no say.

Any symbol or myth that has power can take us out of ourselves, that is, into the transcendent, the ecstasy that Plato called prophetic madness. In *Phaedrus* he wrote of the priestesses at the oracle of Delphi: "It is their madness that accounts for the many benefits they are able to bestow on Greece, both to individuals and to society." The word *madness* is not about pathology but about access to wisdom beyond rational, logic-bound thought or conventional attitudes.

The feminine has a natural ease in moving into the marginal world. Thus, *feminine* means not only female but being beyond the limitations that come with strict adherence to ego, logic, convention, scientific provability, and materialism. The feminine archetype is visionary, so our best intuitions come not from linear reasoning but from feminine energy.

Recently spiritually aware people have come to a greater appreciation of the feminine in the evolution of life. Our reconnection to nature and its ecology is not a coincidence. It is how the mother archetype is calling to us to ready ourselves for personal and planetary birth through her. We can't help but hear her labor pains in all that is happening in the world. A mothering energy wants to free us from the grasp of an ego that denies the presence and necessity of grace.

In infancy and early childhood we experienced, or longed to experience, the safe embrace of our mother's arms. We always remember the felt sense of that in our body all of our life. It is lodged in our personal unconscious as well. We were also born with a lifelong desire for the arms of Mother Nature to hold us. That longing resides in the universal or collective unconscious that we share with all humanity.

Indeed, our experience with our own mother is a metaphor for humanity's relationship to the archetypal mother, offering the holding embrace that comes to us from feminine nurturant powers, both natural and transcendent. Erik Erikson, in *Toys and Reasons: Stages in the Ritualization of Experience,* alludes to this connection. He says that the child seeks in the mother-child bond "the privilege of being lifted up to the very bosom of the divine which, indeed, may be seen graciously to respond with the faint smile of an inclined face [the mother's]." The word *privilege* can be read in this context as a metaphor for spiritual support. Thus, Erikson goes on to say that mother-child time grants a "sense of hallowed presence." Using a religious phrase, he shows that our deepest connections to the feminine nurturant powers are more than merely physical and psychological. They are spiritual, that is, deeper within us and the universe than the mind can measure or plumb.

There is a Greek myth that points to the centrality of nurturance in female consciousness. Lycurgus and Eurydice were the king and queen of Nemea in Greece. When their son Opheltes was born, they were very concerned about his well-being. They asked the oracle at Delphi how to keep him safe and ensure his happiness. The priestess advised them, in the usual paradoxical style of feminine wisdom, not to let him touch the ground before he learned how to walk. The king and queen gave this instruction to the infant's nurse Hypsipyle, and she agreed to be cautious and to hold or cradle him at all times.

One day, with Opheltes in her arms, Hypsipyle was greeted by the Seven Argive generals who were marching to Thebes to engage in battle. They were thirsty and asked her for directions to the nearest spring. Hypsipyle, forgetting her important charge, placed Opheltes in a patch of wild celery while she went to show them the location of the spring. While she was gone, a serpent strangled the unguarded infant.

This myth can be seen to assert the importance of the female archetype as the caring rather than the warring contributor to the collective human story. Hypsipyle forsook her role as nurturer to aid the war effort. This led to sad misfortune because feminine energy was not meant to be oriented toward the furthering of opposition but toward the protection of the helpless. In a contemporary example of the reverse of this, women in the American military have now been "upgraded" to combat and special operations jobs near the front lines.

In a broader context, the ancient myth also shows that war and violence occlude and damage our capacities for caring connection, our central human purpose. This may be why soldiers, both male and female, are apt to lose sight of their humanity in a war and engage in horrendous acts.

However, there is more to the story. The generals were deeply saddened by the tragedy of Opheltes and held funeral games in honor of the young prince. This is thought to be the origin of the Nemean Games, held a year before and a year after the Olympic Games. The winners received a wreath of celery leaves.

The myth thus also shows how the generals—males—paused in their pursuit of war to grieve and memorialize the lost child in a caring way, signifying nurturance as appropriate to both males and females. We actually see this when we notice the many nurturant fathers in today's society. The grace of caring, like every virtue and archetype, is indeed the unlimited potential of all humans. The feminine shows the way, and all of us are given the grace to follow it.

The Materialist Questions

In the patriarchal world there is a lack of trust in—and a suspicion of—feminine powers. We recall Caesar refusing to heed his wife, Calpurnia's, dream not to go to the Senate on the Ides of March. Caesar would not acknowledge the value of a synchronous dream, especially by a woman, over the promptings of his own rational mind and male ego. Denial of the existence of grace by the male ego is ultimately a denial of the power of the feminine.

Some people might see respect for grace as a belief in magic. They might say that grace is only fantasy or religious fiction. They might perceive the special moments in which we exceed our usual limits only as indicators that we have more potential than we had ever imagined and we have finally activated it. They might also say there is no such thing as grace, only felicitous but nonetheless chance occurrences or luck. Chance and luck, however, though haphazard, also seem to imply *some* force or possibility that transcends ordinary consciousness or responsiveness to human control.

Strict scientific materialists adhere to a reductionist style that identifies the mind with what the brain does. They acknowledge nothing as legitimate beyond the provable laws of physics and the potential for accuracy in the human intellect. This confines reality to matter, including mental phenomena such as consciousness. The brain is then merely a conglomerate of neurons that fire in accord with biochemical signals. Consciousness is simply an artifact of that process rather than also something more than can be observed or explained in physiological terms.

The monopoly of reductionist science over all forms of knowledge is not only about adherence to the scientific method in deciding what is or isn't true. Like monotheism, it is about male supremacy. The opposite of feminine in this context is not masculine but materialist.

Reductionist materialism is a denial of the role of feeling, mystery, imagination, and intuition in finding truth. These are associated with female consciousness, suspect because it is a lunar light that is content with ambiguity. The feminine path of knowledge allows for uncertainties. This is unsatisfactory when only male solar clarity is legitimate. Yet, not knowing leads, in the feminine style, not to frustration but to openness, as we see in these lines by Emily Dickinson: "Not knowing when the Dawn will come, / I open every Door."

The hazard in the male need for clear information and secure confirmation is visible in the archetypal myth of Orpheus and his wife Eurydice. When she died, Orpheus sought her in the underworld. This is a metaphor for how someone seeks his feminine self, symbolized by Eurydice, his soul mate in the underworld, which can symbolize the unconscious. Orpheus was given permission by Persephone, queen of the underworld, to retrieve his wife on condition that he not look back at her as they were leaving Hades. Orpheus wanted to be sure Eurydice was indeed behind him, and so he looked back and instantly lost her.

The story seems to say that our masculine need for certitude breaks our connection to our feminine—and spiritual—side. This is the side that can trust ambiguity, transcendence, not knowing, the possibility of grace. Orpheus needed to enter the unconscious with his feminine energies up and running. Then he would not have checked or looked for proof—the actions of the scientist. Such actions have their place, but not in the depth dimensions of ourselves. In our true nature, the realm of the higher self, our masculine skill set does not serve. Rather, we can only enter and then rest in uncertainty until something opens on its own. That is the skill we learn as we respect and respond to grace.

The following chart may help us see the distinctions between intellectual and imaginal styles. They often reflect traditional male and female differences too.

The Mental-Intellectual Style	*Our Imagination*
Insists on defining	Is comfortable with ambiguity
Sees pairs of opposites that battle one another	Perceives paradoxical combinations
Acknowledges the standard dimensions	Recognizes infinite possibilities
Remains rational at all times	Honors the imaginal
Reckons everything as either/or	Has room for both/and
Divides and analyzes	Continually notices more and more unity and synthesis
Explains and controls	Makes room for mystery
Is limited to what makes sense and can be proven	Believes that there are realities that go beyond the scope of science
Is mediated mostly by the left hemisphere of the brain	Is comfortable in the right hemisphere of the brain
Sees problems and focuses on finding solutions and answers	Wonders at mystery and tolerates not knowing the answers or having solutions
Sees oneself as an expert	Sees oneself as a beginner

The Mental-Intellectual Style	*Our Imagination*
Trusts only effort	Trusts in and is open to grace
Omits or is unconvinced about anything dubbed transcendent	Honors a transcendent dimension in ordinary reality
Seeks sunlight clarity	Is content with moonlight glow

A More Inclusive Alternative

Physicists Paul Davies and John Gribbin, in their book *The Matter Myth,* propose an open-ended alternative to scientific materialism, based on quantum theory: "Newton's deterministic machine was replaced by a shadowy and paradoxical conjunction of waves and particles, governed by the laws of chance.... Solid matter dissolves away.... Quantum physics undermines materialism because it reveals that matter has far less 'substance' than we might believe."

Recent books critical of religious belief from Richard Dawkins, Sam Harris, and Christopher Hitchens take a stand against belief in the transcendent. Using a masculine-way-of-knowing format, they disparage religious doctrines as illusory, since they cannot be proven by strictly scientific tools of investigation. It seems that physical, empirically testable reality is all the reality there is for these authors. This is not only a disparagement of religion. Their view annuls the validity of the feminine dimension in understanding ourselves and our world.

The scientific perspective is certainly useful in a laboratory or in research. But to relate it to all areas of human experience takes faith, since that broad an application would take tools that science does not have. How ironic that faith becomes an unrecognized tool in the materialists' kit.

The feminine style of contentment with the indefinite and undefined fits with Buddhist teaching about emptiness. People and things lack a fixed core, an identifiable, definable reality. Everything is open, empty, not discrete and freestanding but dynamically and interactively flowing. This means that entities are not things but relationships, interconnections. There are no beings, only interbeing. Hamlet's real question was "To be *with* or not to be." William James points to the grace element: "The religious question is primarily a question of life, of *living or not living in the higher union* [my italics] which opens itself to us as a gift."

What we can call the sense of self is consciousness of or an experience of a personal identity. But that self-identity keeps changing as it interacts with other identities. It is not stable but ever shape-shifting in flow with people and circumstance. Thus we humans are a single *connected* self. That is the self—in each of us—receiving ongoing grace within the family of humanity.

The special moments in which we individuals receive a grace show how the universe loves to become personal, to incarnate itself in time and space. Yet this happens so that all can benefit, since we are not isolated individuals but are intricately connected. We can also see that *bodhicitta,* individual enlightenment meant to be shared, perfectly reflects this wisdom of human-communal rather than ruggedly individual existence.

The feminine style makes more room for this option than does the male bias toward definitive distinctions and divisions. It is intriguing that in modern physics there is agreement that objects are not made of mass but are waves of relatedness, just where the feminine is at home.

Buddha is sometimes described as smiling because he has noticed something that others have not seen. The Prajnaparamita Sutra states: "It is never without an illuminating reason that the enlightened ones manifest their cosmic smile." We smile when we notice grace, often not visible or believable to others. We smile, not scornfully, but to include and invite them into our joyous realization that grace is at work everywhere.

Three Realities

To understand where grace can stand in the full scheme of things, we can look at three of the many forms of reality. This set of distinctions offers an alternative to the strictly materialist view.

There are *material realities* mediated through our senses. For instance, people, places, and things come through to us through sight, sound, taste, smell, and touch. The design of material realities is visible in how they display. Grace comes through these realities but is not itself a material reality.

There are *immaterial experiences* not caused by us but that happen to us, for instance, chance, luck, coincidence, accidents. They are in the design of the universe and are displayed at special times and in individual circumstances. Grace is in this category, since it is a happening that is not caused by us but can be mediated through material realities and immaterial qualities.

There are *immaterial qualities* such as thoughts, feelings, personal traits, beliefs, aptitudes, imagination. They are not tangible, but they do have physical concomitants in our brain. They combine design and display. For instance, we have the capacity for courage built into the design—set of capacities—of our psyche, and it can be displayed in our actions. A grace gives the extra boost that can actualize an inner design of wholeness that transcends any derring-do the ego can muster. Disney's Pinocchio can show male bravado and be brave enough to rescue his father from the whale. But to be a real boy he needs the touch of the female Blue Fairy. How many of us men dare to admit that we need something from the feminine to be truly masculine? Can we trust our masculinity enough to acknowledge our need for graces that only feminine energy can give us?

In Catholicism, one of the titles of Mary is Our Lady of Grace. There is a long-standing appeal in the image of the Madonna offering graces to humanity, as did her predecessor the Great Mother goddess. For instance, in Catholic tradition, Mary appeared to Saint Catherine Labouré in nineteenth-century France. In the vision, Mary was standing in the grace-giving pose of the ancient goddesses, her palms facing forward. On each finger was a gold ring. Some of the rings emitted rays of light, graces from the divine feminine to humanity. When Saint Catherine asked why some rings did not emit light, Mary replied: "Those are the graces people have not yet asked me for."

Sadly, we don't dare ask for the graces that await us so copiously. We don't ask often enough or for enough from the feminine powers. We recall the words of Thomas Merton in his poem "To the Immaculate Virgin on a Winter Night": "Where in the world has any voice prayed to you, Lady, for the peace that's in your power?" Notice the similarity between that prayer and this passage from the Prajnaparamita Sutra: "The bodhisattvas will always maintain a motherly mind, consecrated to the constant protection, education, and maturing of conscious beings, inviting and guiding them along the path of all-embracing love." Bodhisattvas are enlightened beings who keep coming back to earth to help us. The recurrent appearances of Mary throughout history have that same style. They can also be seen to be the feminine arising to counteract the one-sidedness of masculine domination in our science, religion, political system, and culture. The feminine style of knowing is all-sided. It embraces both fact and symbol.

Our fear of or contempt for the feminine restricts our access to the transcendent. Prejudice against women—as happens in so many societies today—is thus contrary not only to equal rights but to an equal chance to evolve by accessing the transcendent. It seems appropriate to conclude this thought with a courageous statement by President Jimmy Carter when he left the Southern Baptist Convention in 2000. He understood that patriarchal churches that do not affirm the equality of women thereby implicitly underwrite and grant permission to men everywhere to engage in violence against them.

> Male religious leaders have had, and still have, an option to interpret holy teachings either to exalt or subjugate women. They have, for their own selfish ends, overwhelmingly chosen the latter. Their continuing choice provides the foundation or justification for much of the pervasive persecution and abuse of women throughout the world. This is in clear violation not only of the Universal Declaration of Human Rights but also of the teachings of Jesus Christ, the Apostle Paul, Moses and the prophets, Muhammad, and founders of other great religions, all of whom have called for proper and equitable treatment of all the children of God. It is time we had the courage to challenge these views.

The Shadow of the Feminine

Throughout this book we find references to the dark side. *Dark* is a metaphor for the dangerous, the scary, the challenging negative impulses we keep "in the dark," though they hold so much creative energy.

Grace works to create balance. Dark and light are held in balance; they do not have to be oppositional. Think of bread making. The light is required for kneading, the darkness for rising. In painting a picture, we work on a canvas in the light, but that does not represent the full creative process. We also let an idea for a canvas incubate in the dark recesses of our imagination before we take up the brushes and colors.

An example of a holder of the dark feminine divine is the goddess Kali in the Hindu pantheon. She is the mother goddess, yet she is devouring and destructive. Kali wears a necklace of skulls, symbolizing how she disposes of our personas and head trips. Her role is to challenge us on the spiritual path with disturbing afflictions and questions. Ultimately her purpose is to make us stronger and more realistic about our limitations so that the power of her grace can come into full focus in our lives.

The dark-goddess figure in stories escorts the hero into the dark night of the soul. She hurls the hero more deeply into the pit of chaos and the startling dismantling of his powers. Only there can he locate the special clue he needs to take his next step or to find the key that opens him to the real meaning of his struggle.

We see examples of the dark feminine in nature. The mother bear gently cherishes her cub but defends it fiercely; her caring is warlike in its ferocity. Thus she is the bearer of light in her nurturance of her young and the cudgel of the dark when she defends them. We see a combination or, rather, coincidence of apparent opposites. Both nurturance and aggression are necessary features of a full archetype, such as that of mother. And whatever is true of mother energy is true of nature.

Sometimes the dark feminine shows us our own darkness. We don't easily believe we have destructive power in us. Our bias and fear keep awareness of our own dark feminine energies hidden from us. We tend to see them in female figures around us, for example, the difficult wife, the controlling mother, the demanding boss. In reality we contain the whole human spectrum of behavior. Once we acknowledge this, we cease projecting our own darkness onto women. We are no longer afraid of them because we are no longer afraid of ourselves.

In our society, we are not taught to expect a confrontation with the shadow side of the feminine in others or in ourselves. We do not learn how to face it nose to nose and benefit from it. Our task is then to find it in ourselves. Odysseus in the *Odyssey,* by his own slyness, finds a way to outwit the Sirens, personifications of the dark feminine power to destroy. They, by the way, are also symbols of how the shadow side of the feminine lures the male ego to submersion in the waters of dissolution. But this death is a baptism into a new birth. The dark feminine dips the ego in egolessness, the font of fearlessness. Is this the gift we are evading?

After facing the dark feminine, we gain the gift of more knowledge of ourselves, especially of how both the dark and the light in us can be trusty resources on the journey. The Greek goddess Persephone showed us how when she embraced her destiny to live in the underworld for half the year and on the earth for the other half. She accepted the dark as equal with the light. She showed all of us that we need both. Animals know how to do this; they can hibernate, grow in the dark. So does bread and so can we.

6

Graces on the Dark Paths

It takes just such evil and painful things for the great eman-
cipation to occur.

—Friedrich Nietzsche, *Human, All Too Human*

In the preceding chapter we considered the dark side of the feminine.
We now look at the shadow in our personal and collective life. We
see how grace can appear not only as a burst of light but also as an encounter with the dark.

With a positive view of the shadow, we can regard dark events as a
furthering of our evolution through experiences of destruction and in-
security. This path in the dusk is uncertain, and the dangers are myriad.
We are challenged to find our safety and security in affliction as well as
in comfort.

In stories, the afflicting forces are the people or circumstances that
attempt to wreck the heroine's chances of fulfilling her mission. They
are the unfriendly powers that upset the heroine's plans, that render
her temporarily immobile, that prevent her from moving along
smoothly on the path, that keep placing obstacles in her way. Yet, ultimately, the afflicting forces serve important positive ends. They show
the heroine her need for assistance beyond her own powers. This assistance in heroic-journey stories often comes from unusual, weak, or

utterly improbable sources—like the mouse who saves the elephant in the Aesop fable.

The afflicting forces help the heroine marshal her powers, inducing her to build her strength in response to the grace she receives. Thus, in the long run, the heroine gains from the villainy she confronts because it reveals unexpected resources and increases her warrior powers. The obstacles pave the way toward victory. Marianne Moore proposed that Hercules "was hindered to succeed" in her poem "The Paper Nautilus."

Afflicting forces help all of us on a daily basis. The person in our lives who most upsets us may offer a reflection of an undiscovered part of ourselves. He helps us know ourselves at a deeper level than our ego has previously permitted. Luke Skywalker comes to realize that the one he opposed as his darkest enemy is his own father, that is, his own DNA, his own flesh and blood—another side of himself. Luke discovers his own negative shadow, the disturbing dimension that seemed separate from or opposed to him. The comic-strip character Pogo said it well: "We have met the enemy and he is us."

In our own shadow work, we too notice that what is totally visible and offensive to us in other people is often an invisible part of ourselves. Jung referred to letting go of projecting our shadow onto others as a crucial step in the integration of ego and self, our individuation. In the example of Luke Skywalker, his realization that he is connected to the dark side is also a realization that he is royal. This is the alchemy of our humanity: the highest benefit emerges from the least promising quarter—just like the workings of grace.

There are two afflicting forces that arouse shadow energy in our lives: calamity and chaos.

Calamity

Carl Jung, in an interview in the December 1961 issue of *Good Housekeeping,* said: "God is the name by which I designate all things that cross my path violently and recklessly, all things which upset my subjective views, plans, and intentions and change the course of my life for better or worse."

The negative shadow can be a vehicle of grace to us through adverse events. Examples are illnesses, accidents, catastrophes, losses, a collapse of our powers or skills.

Since every event offers a built-in opportunity for growth, there is a gift dimension to our calamities. This is another coincidence of opposites, another wonderfully sanguine paradox built into the very structure of the human story. We can also apply the built-in-opportunity model to our own capacities: Within our capacity to love is the grace to show it in new and unexpected ways.

The German poet Friedrich Hölderlin wrote: "Danger itself invites the rescuing power." There is something inherent in threat and danger that assures us grace is not far behind—it's even included in them. We feel fear, yet from the grace perspective, we can actually feel confident within the fear.

In terms of the heroic-journey archetype, it is especially in unwelcome events that assisting forces reach out to us. The afflicting forces in calamities and adverse events are thus revealed to be the shadow side of assisting forces. Like all apparent opposites, they can work together. This is what makes our journey optimistic.

Here is an example of how grace works in a rescuing way when our usually trusty powers collapse. In his book *The Mountains of California,* John Muir describes climbing Mount Ritter in the high Sierras at an elevation of 12,800 feet. He was trying to scale a rock face when his mountaineering skills failed him and he became unable to move: "My doom appeared fixed. I must fall . . . to the glacier below. . . . But this terrible eclipse lasted only a moment, when life blazed forth again with preternatural clearness. I seemed suddenly to become possessed of a new sense. The other self, bygone experiences, Instinct, or Guardian Angel—call it what you will—came forward and assumed control. Then my trembling muscles became firm again . . . and my limbs moved with a positiveness and precision with which I seemed to have nothing at all to do. Had I been borne aloft upon wings, my deliverance could not have been more complete. . . . I found a way without effort, and soon stood upon the topmost crag in the blessed light."

When grace happens, we feel that we are receiving something, not actively pursuing or acting but being acted upon. We notice this realization in these statements by Muir:

"I seemed suddenly to become possessed of a new sense."

"The other self . . . came forward and assumed control."

"My trembling muscles became firm again . . . and my limbs moved."

"Borne aloft upon wings."

"My deliverance could not have been more complete."

"I found a way without effort."

Most of us imagine that grace works only on the bright side of the human equation. We reject the possibility of a gift dimension in danger, illness, loss, rejection, abandonment, or inauspicious events. Such a gift may take years to shape itself into more depth, character, and compassion in how we live our lives—examples of grace at work.

We might be clinging to the superstition cherished by the entitled ego: "All will turn out for the best for me." That does not always happen—John Muir's experience notwithstanding. We cannot say we will not be faced with more than we can handle or that tragedy will not occur. Sometimes, we are forced to experience something beyond our capacity to assimilate. We suffer then from a long post-traumatic reaction, sometimes never fully resolvable. All we can trust is that every event in life, no matter how painful, offers us an opportunity to practice mindfulness and loving-kindness—sources of spiritual growth even though not capable of healing all wounds.

Our challenge is always to appreciate a gift advantage in any circumstance, especially when its hidden opportunity is not immediately evident. Shakespeare, in Sonnet 120, gives us a glimpse of a sunny consequence that can arise, for instance, from unwelcome hurts: "That you were once unkind befriends [helps] me now."

Here is an example of finding grace in an unwelcome and devastating event: We lose our job and relationship, and life as we know it falls apart. Our self-esteem suffers; our finances are in disarray; we feel unsupported and lonely. We see no grace in what has happened to us. Yet, somehow, we come through the losses and perhaps find a whole new direction in life. Only then can we look back and recognize the gift dimension in the events. For example, being fired might become a gift of spurs for our ride into working for ourselves in some creative way.

If we do not come through the loss with something new but keep losing, we find out how brittle life and success really are. So we still gain, because we have encountered the spiritual truth of how the world is shaped and how fragile is its stability.

It is only despair that can blind us to the gift momentum in an experience. The event cannot come through to us as a grace until we open to what can bloom next, no matter how miniscule the benefit or how long it takes us to notice, receive, or be animated by it.

The grace in dark events does not emerge magically. It can happen only when we join in the forward movements of grace and march into them fully. Then we more easily resurrect ourselves from our catastrophes. Thus, grace is a gift potential in what happens. When it offers itself, it is up to us to take advantage of that offering. We begin to do this when we give up being victims of circumstance, when we honestly ask: "What can I make of what happened? How can I work with this event so that it opens me to something new? How can this serve me and others?" Part of getting to this point is cultivating the trusting attitude "If it happened, it must hold an opportunity." As Benjamin Franklin said: "The things that hurt instruct."

Void and Chaos

A sudden loss of what we hold dear can shake the foundations on which our life is built. We lose our frame of reference, what gave it meaning, what upheld us in the quakes and storms. We find ourselves suspended in a void, naked and vulnerable, no place to stand or hide, no standpoint to take or defend, detached from support and security. This terrifying void may be a catalyst for the grace that allows us to leap beyond the impermanence that looked permanent, the precariousness that looked fixed. We become free of illusion *because of* how far we fell. Something turns us to surrender to the givens of life just as they are. Something makes us realize there will be no exceptions made for us. And somehow, we stand into that truth, never to be afraid again.

Thomas Merton wrote in his journal of November 1952: "Suspended entirely from God's mercy, I am content that anything should happen." This is the attitude of openness, a yes to what is and what may next arise no matter how unpromising the present turn of events. This is why a yes to what is carries us across the threshold of fear.

For many of us, every truly meaningful change in our lives can be traced to an event that threw us for a loop, turned everything upside down, hurled us into disarray. These chaotic events can be configured as positive or negative based on how we interpret and respond to them: We were laid off, lost our partner or home, became addicted, had a mental breakdown. Any of these things can become something positive for us in time. Any of them can be appreciated eventually as a grace in disguise when we lift its frightening mask. We can see that opening to grace takes freedom from the belief that unwelcome events are nothing but bad.

With trust in grace, obstacles that lay waste the path do not stop or stymie us. They increase our enthusiasm for what may bloom next and they give us the eyes to see it, no matter how microscopic it might be. In any case, wherever there is chaos, we can trust that a holy spirit is brooding, as the first page of the Bible asserts.

According to the second law of thermodynamics, isolated systems have a built-in entropy: they tend to break down and decay with time. But then something new emerges. New forms do not appear when all is ordered and stable. They arise from novel interactions within chaos, from a breakdown of a system that has nowhere to go but out of its old form into something altogether new. When everything falls apart, we are in the best position for innovations to arise. This is the grace that in religious terms is called resurrection, the rearising (literally) that signifies new life from death.

According to the law of syntropy, natural things continually reach new levels of organization and harmony. The properties of syntropy are therefore future attracting, as is the evolution of all living things. It is an anticipatory and optimistic reality that ensures the possibility of order, not just the disorder of entropy, which is future ending.

The notion of order from chaos is, however, a traditionally masculine aspiration. The spirit of grace that broods over chaos is the feminine, which is not necessarily predictable and orderly. Grace happens both in syntropy and entropy. We find opportunity both in what attracts us to a flourishing future and in what disturbs us about what has to come to an end.

Grace is not all sweetness and light. It can occur in uncontrollable, wild, passionate flashes that can be disturbing to those who require orderliness. The style of grace is the same style as that of creativity. It has a loose and erotic quality that may feel threatening to the ego that seeks to keep everything under control. Once again, the more we free ourselves from inhibiting fear, the more the path to grace opens.

It is grace that awakens our inclination to bring new order from chaos or to find great advantages in a minor boon. It is grace that awakens us to ever more splendid possibilities. This is how we gain hope in the unfolding human adventure we are here to enjoy. Hope happens when we have an unobstructed vision of prospects. Hope is vision that transcends what we have heretofore been able to reach.

Some images from Buddhism can help us understand what we have been exploring: Some Buddhist deities are pictured as blissful, some as wrathful. Avalokiteshvara, the bodhisattva of compassion, beams compassion, reaching out to us with many arms. Manjushri, the remover of illusions, on the other hand, emits terror and wrath. His sword is meant to cut through our attachments. Both are trying to help us. Both are on and at our side. They are not literal beings but aspects of our own deep psyche. We see the blissful side of the deities/ourselves when we are open and the wrathful side when we need to be opened. Our life is a continuous relay between those two possibilities.

In the Face of Evil

> The people found grace in the desert.
>
> —JEREMIAH 31:2

We have been seeing that suffering, albeit unwelcome, keeps appearing in the human story as a difficult but reliable threshold to grace. But how is there an opportunity for growth in truly evil events such as genocide? There are predators who are so possessed by the dark side that they take away the freedom or lives of others. How can that have any gift dimension?

Grace is a delicate reality that has little chance to assert itself tangibly in the face of inescapable evil. It is hard to see grace at work in genocide, death camps, harsh persecutions, torture, terrorist attacks, hate crimes, rapes, child abuse, war. It is certainly a formidable challenge to trust the presence of grace when the collective shadow of evil arises so robustly and inescapably. Yet again and again in our human story, someone finds the light of grace, however flickering, even in the darkest dark. We see this in the prayer found near the body of a dead child in the women's concentration camp at Ravensbrück in 1945, where ninety-two thousand women and children died: "O God, remember not only the men and women of good will but also those of ill will. But do not remember only the suffering they have inflicted on us. Remember the fruits we bought thanks to this suffering: our comradeship, our loyalty, our humility, and the courage, generosity, and greatness of heart that has grown out of all this pain. And when they come to judgment let all the fruits we have gained become their forgiveness." Yes, grace can touch any of us and make it possible not to have to hate those causing our pain. This is the victory of grace over evil.

Saint Paul wrote to the Romans that "where sin abounded, grace abounded more" (Rom. 5:20). Trust in grace means believing, against all odds and evidence, that somehow there has been and will always be more grace than danger, more grace than evil, more grace than despair. The fact that love survives all fires and lights them all makes that a certainty.

The Austrian psychiatrist Viktor Frankl was interned in a Nazi concentration camp. In his book *Man's Search for Meaning*, he wrote of a grueling forced march in the dead of winter. In that extreme moment of suffering, he suddenly recalled his wife's loving face and found consolation. This is his description of that moment of grace: "A thought transfixed me: for the first time in my life I saw the truth . . . that . . . the salvation of man is through love and in love. I understood how a man who has nothing left in this world still may know bliss, be it only for a brief moment, in the contemplation of his beloved."

Frankl's experience evokes the age-old mystery of human suffering. Proponents of the New Age style of spirituality sometimes declare that everything happens for a reason. This may be magical thinking rather than an adult yes to the way life is. It may be a way of consoling ourselves, of dulling the thud of the unalterable given of life that pain and injustice are in store for all of us. We don't want to believe that sometimes pain is meaningless and senseless, since then it hurts us more and makes us doubt that there's a silver lining to the cloud.

A mature spiritual alternative might be the acknowledgment that pain may not have a meaning or reason but that it does have a function in human life. For instance, Frankl's suffering served to arouse his hope about the power of love in the human story. Finding hope is invoking the presence of those who have reassured us in the course of our lives. Through our pain we are offered the opportunity to find out how life works, that no one of us is exempt from its harsh blows. Through our pain we are given the opportunity to practice mindfulness and loving-kindness. Because of our pain, we can even redeem ourselves and others by the grace of forgiveness. We will never understand the mystery of suffering. Yet we can learn to live with it and cross the threshold it presents into acceptance of reality. Once we see suffering as a threshold to grace, we know it need not render us immobile. The dark side of humanity—"man's inhumanity to man"—will never go away. Meeting it in the light of spiritual adulthood, acknowledging its presence in ourselves, may not make it palatable, but it does make it understandable. Our commitment to the practice of nonviolence in our own lives and our compassion for those at the mercy of the dark side are the spiritual options always ready and waiting for us. We might even embrace the over-the-top challenge to care about those who inflict unconscionable pain and aspire to or pray for their conversion. That would be a trust in the power of grace indeed.

We have all noticed two inescapable realities that dismay and irritate us. The first is the dark side of humanity that we have been discussing in this section. The second is the unappealing set of givens that life presents to us. For instance, we notice the givens of dissatisfaction and disappointment that meet us again and again in our experiences and relationships. To accept the shadow and givens of life matter of factly as "the way it is" takes practice. However, to accept them without grousing or becoming cynical about life and relationships takes grace. Radically accepting the shadow and the givens with equanimity and without complaint means that grace has become a container holding our hearts in perfect harmony with the human condition.

In the face of disappointment, hurt, and betrayal, our instinct may be to resent others and retaliate against them. It is grace that moves us to go beyond—to transcend—those primitive options. To forgive is to let go of resentment and ill will in favor of goodwill, to let go of holding a grudge in favor of wanting the best for the other, to let go of the need for retaliation in favor of the desire for reconciliation. We can work toward those goals in psychotherapy or in spiritual practices. However, most of us discover that when forgiveness happens in us, it feels like a grace-impelled shift rather than a result of effort. We set the stage when we take responsibility for our feelings, but grace brings down the final curtain on our resentments.

This discussion of forgiveness shows us that an experience of grace actually indicates that a quantum leap in evolution is happening within our hearts. We move from a primitive reaction—for example, retaliation—to an evolved choice such as reconciliation. We move from what divides to what unites, from separation to connection. This is how grace transcends our Cro-Magnon past and shifts us into the spiritual consciousness we see in Christ and the Buddha.

While I was writing this book, the terrible shootings in Newtown, Connecticut, occurred. I fell into a long slump in the ensuing days. It was a combination of grief and despondency. I was, during this period, slated to give a talk to a meditation group. One of the questions put to me was "Do you think the world is getting any better?" I had not planned a reply, but I heard myself saying this in all sincerity: "When I think of what happened in Connecticut, I say no. When I look at all of you, I say yes." I appreciate that it was grace that gave me those words.

In our despair, against our will, comes wisdom through the awful grace of God.

—AESCHYLUS, *Agamemnon*

7

Grace in Religion

It was you, O Lord, who accomplished all this in us.

—ISAIAH 26:12

A strong man is not saved by his great strength. . . . Our soul waits for God who is our help and our shield.

—PSALM 33:16, 22

Just wait, soon you too will find rest.

—JOHANN WOLFGANG VON GOETHE,
"THE WANDERER'S SECOND NIGHT SONG"

It was religion that preserved the concept of grace throughout the centuries. Grace was considered the cause of a gift or miracle and a sense of a divine presence in the world. We still hear the phrase *God willing*. This is a way of acknowledging a need for the ingredient of grace in our enterprises. Grace in this context is beyond our control and necessary for good things to happen, a common understanding of grace in religious traditions. Human efforts are considered insufficient. Faith is in help from a God who grants supernatural grace.

Supernatural is a term commonly used to refer to the transcendent. In Ken Wilber's view, as stated in *Eye to Eye*, however: "Supernatural is simply the next natural step in overall or higher development and evolution." We might take a cue from Wilber and say that grace is an interior reality within us and the universe and that what is natural is also transcendent, that is, aimed at higher development and evolution.

The German theologian Karl Rahner seems to move in this direction when he teaches that grace, already and always given to everyone, has created a permanent upgrading of our human nature. He calls this feature of our being "a supernatural existential," using Martin Heidegger's phrase. This means that grace is an ego-transcending quality, the divine built into every human person. Rahner rejects the possibility of a nongraced human, whether or not he or she is religious or even spiritually oriented. In this theological view, we are fully human, more than an ego, because of grace.

Rahner even proposed that grace is actually the same as the healthy tendency in us to become whole. He saw grace as whatever in us wants to transcend ego limits, to detach from fear and craving, to let go of self-absorption, to release our fully creative self. Our inherent inclination to such transcendence of ego is how grace comes through to us. Thus, grace does not destroy our ego. It works with ego, supplementing its positive efforts and taming its negative inclinations.

Ancient Religion

In myth, grace often comes in the form of assistance from the gods and goddesses or through their intervention. Heroes are given the gifts of courage, sagacity, success. Sometimes the gods or goddesses also intervene to save the hero from making a mistake. In the *Iliad,* as Achilles draws his sword to smite his commander, Agamemnon, Athena, standing behind him invisibly, catches him by the hair to prevent him from completing his rash deed. Athena is a metaphor for the feminine power of the grace of wisdom.

When a hero was victorious in battle, he ascribed his triumph to divine help. This was not only an expression of gratitude but a way of preserving himself from hubris, the arrogance of a self-congratulating ego, the claim to self-sufficiency, the denial of the role of divine help in his success. Hubris is the primary tragic flaw that leads to the downfall of the hero.

It is important to acknowledge that the erroneous, tragic, or negative deeds of great personages in mythology were likewise often ascribed to divine influence. For instance, it was Aphrodite who induced Helen to fall in love with Paris so that their elopement could instigate the Trojan War. This is a way of showing the heft of the feminine dark side.

Grace is pure gift. Thus, in Greek mythology, Plutus, the god of riches, was struck blind by Zeus so that he would distribute fortune to people irrespective of merit or favoritism. This shows symbolically how grace is given to us without respect to accomplishment.

The Romans engaged in religious rituals to bless myriad activities from breast-feeding to the spreading of manure for crops. The people were acknowledging the power of the divine in nature and showing their respect and gratitude for how it was helping them thrive. They were also acknowledging a sense of protection from the many perils and insecurities in the world around them.

Romans were aware that the gods could as easily harm as help them, so this was not only about seeking graces. The religious rituals had an element of appeasement. This sense of the divine as both rewarding and punitive is a projection of the primitive ego, not yet matured into full spiritual consciousness. It's the state of mind in which God is like us at the ego level rather than at the level of our higher self, our true nature that does not punish but loves.

In his process theology, the philosopher Alfred North Whitehead mused on the role of God in a world of change: since God is love and love changes, God is continually evolving. Traditional theology emphasizes divine nature as immovable, absolute, independent. But that can't be the God of love, because love is moving, evolving, and interdependent. Nor can it be the God of grace, since grace is continually moving. God is then the grace-giving love that moves the world, us, and the other stars, as Dante said.

For Whitehead, God does not exercise power by force or coercion but by the allurements of love. God's caring is how divine grace reaches out to humans. This is a way of saying that grace is not forced on us but offered to us the way a lover offers her love. The prophet Hosea refers to how God loved the people of Israel: "I drew them with cords of human kindness, with ties of love" (Hosea 11:4).

To understand Whitehead's view, we can look at realizations from contemporary liberal theology: God is not an individual, not a being. God is the depth dimension of being by which beings transcend their usual limitations.

For instance, love transcends itself when it becomes consistently unconditional in its expression and universal in its extent. That transcendent quality, that abundant fullness of what love can be, is what is meant by God in us. Thus the phrase "God is love" means that wherever love is unconditional and universal it *is* divine presence.

The transcendent—divine—dimension of reality is not only love but also our longing for it. When we long to be loved unconditionally, we are longing for the divine. The fullness that love can reach and our longing to be reached by it is *how* God as love meets us in grace.

Other Traditions

Grace in Hindu scriptures is akin to *kripa,* what it takes to be fully realized. *Anugraha* can refer to grace as a benediction. Realization means release from the cycle of lifetimes, finally free of karmic debt. But we cannot achieve such fulfillment on our own without assistance from beyond ourselves.

In the Bhagavad Gita, Krishna says to Arjuna: "Those who worship me with love live in me and I come to life in them" (9:29). The yoga of devotion, *bhakti,* requires a total surrender of our ego so that all that we are is offered to the divine. This leads to freedom from attachment. The surrender of the soul to God the Beloved is the aim of Hindu *bhakti.* This devotion requires grace, which Krishna promises to give unfailingly: "You shall overcome all difficulties through my grace" (18:58; Eknath Easwaran translation). Thus, a devotional relationship to the divine also becomes an access to grace. We notice in the quotations above, by the way, that love is acknowledged as our most cherished grace. In Islam, grace is necessary for entrance into paradise. We cannot achieve salvation by our own merits unaided by the mercy of Allah. The most often-repeated phrase in Islam is "Bismi 'Lâhi'r-Rahmâni'r-Rahîm" (In the Name of God, the Compassionate, the Merciful). *Ar-Rahmân* refers to mercy as the inherent nature of God. *Ar-Rahîm* is the compassion and mercy when it reaches into time and space in the form of grace for us humans.

We find this reference in the Koran regarding the free and arbitrary element of grace: "By his command He sends the Spirit to any of his servants as he pleases" (40:15). This fits with the perennial understanding of grace as freely, arbitrarily given, not distributed equally but nonetheless available in some form to everyone.

In the Hebrew Bible grace is often translated as *chen*. This word connotes favor, charm, moral kindness, kindly disposition: "Noah found favor with the Lord" (Gen. 6:8).

Grace is also directly connected to how God loves us and how we love God. It was clear to ancient peoples that their God was not reliably successful in helping them grow crops or win wars. They settled for a God who offered the gift of caring about them. Hence we read in Exodus: "God looked on the Israelites and was concerned about them" (2:25). This provided a comfort that felt like a personal and protective accompaniment. We see this metaphor in the Biblical story of Tobias, who was accompanied on a journey by a supposed family member who was actually the archangel Raphael, the healer. Symbolically, the "family member" signifies that the accompaniment feels familiar and part of himself. The healer as "accompanying" signifies how accompaniment itself has a healing quality. We recall in the Twenty-Third Psalm that the phrase "I will fear no evil" is joined to "for you are with me." Indeed, the sense of accompaniment, of a reliable alliance, makes us fearless. We keep noticing the direct connection between trust in grace and freedom from fear.

> The believer in nonviolence has deep faith in the future. He knows that in his struggle for justice he has cosmic companionship. There is a creative force in this universe that

works to bring the disconnected aspects of reality into a harmonious whole.

—MARTIN LUTHER KING JR., *Stride Toward Freedom*

A Christian Perspective

In Christian theology grace is a gift from God and is related to faith. Saint Paul summarizes this way: "For it is by grace you have been saved, through faith—and this is not from yourselves, it is the gift of God—not by works [our efforts] so no one can boast [engage in hubris]" (Eph. 2:7–9). Because of grace, we no longer rely on the tool kit of ego but on a power beyond it. Thus, faith is trust in grace. Here is an example: When Saracens broke into her convent, Saint Clare (1194–1253) prayed for the nuns in her charge: "Protect your servants because I cannot." The intruders departed without stealing anything or harming anyone. We also notice that the faith behind the prayer is what worked. Words of prayers do not cause change; only faith does. And faith is itself a gift of grace.

Karl Rahner, in *Foundations of Christian Faith,* expands on this view when he sees grace as necessary even to be able to receive grace: "God's self-communication as offer [grace] is also the necessary condition which makes its acceptance possible."

We see this same concept in the second of the twelve steps of Alcoholics Anonymous: "We came to believe that a Power greater than ourselves could restore us to sanity." The phrase "came to believe" rather than "chose to believe" has the sense of being led to the belief. It takes grace to find grace.

In the mystical view, grace is the infallible affirmation of the divine in the human, that is, the presence of a transcendent reality in the depth of our humanity. The focus is not on God as the giver of gifts but as the gift itself. Grace is the way the divine lives in us, the gift dimension of our being and experience. When we find grace—God—in our true nature, we have found mature faith.

In Christian theology, grace is an *unsolicited* gift from God: "For the grace of God has appeared for the salvation of all men [without our asking]" (Titus 2:11). Thus, grace from God is a continuous gift energy—God energy—in all that happens to us.

The mystery of grace is the central focus of Christian theology. Grace is the gratuitous love God has for us. Grace is what makes it possible for the presence of God in the world to be experienced. Grace becomes real to us when it is felt, experienced. This is why it is not a dollop added to our being but a permeating of our being by love.

God's grace is unconditional mercy, that is, it is not based on merit but on love for us. Grace comes to the world in a powerful way by the incarnation, death, and resurrection of Christ. God creates the world out of an outpouring of love and sends Jesus to us as the natural conclusion of that outpouring. God wants contact with and response from us and freely gives us the grace to do so.

Grace completes what is needed for salvation—eternal life with God—since our own efforts are insufficient for so great a result. Saint Paul therefore writes: "He [God] said unto me, 'My grace is sufficient for thee, for [my] strength is made perfect in [your] weakness.' Most gladly therefore will I [Paul] rather glory in my infirmities" (2 Cor. 12:9). Saint Paul seems to be saying that it is precisely his deficiencies that draw divine grace to him. It is not accomplishments but room for grace that makes humans appealing to the God of grace.

The word *grace* is used more than 150 times in the New Testament. It is a translation of the Greek word *charis,* favor, that which brings joy or good fortune. In pagan times, *charis* was applied to art, athletics, people, and the special gifts or miraculous powers bestowed by the gods. A miracle is generally defined as an extraordinary and unusual event, from a divine source, that suspends nature's laws and has beneficent results.

The word *charis* is related to the word *charisma,* which means "gracious gift." Since grace urges us to transcend ourselves, it is not a personal gift but one meant to be shared. Grace is social. Thus, Saint Thomas Aquinas called grace both "operative" in and for us and "cooperative" in and for others. In this combination we see a similarity to the Buddhist concept of *bodhicitta.*

There is in this business more than nature
Was ever conduct of.
—WILLIAM SHAKESPEARE, *The Tempest*

Gift, State, and Means of Transformation

There are three instances of grace in the traditional Christian theological view: the gift of grace, the state of grace, and the means of grace. The gift of grace is conversion, the inclination to turn toward God in faith. In the state of grace we maintain our connection to God by prayer and virtue. The means of grace are the actions, rituals, or practices that make for, but cannot cause, union with God.

In the Christian perspective, conversion, turning toward God and godliness, is a grace. The theologian Raimundo Pannikar, in *Blessed Simplicity*, writes: "[It is] not by thinking . . . or desiring . . . but because of an urge, the fruit of an experience that eventually leads us to change [to] break from something in this life . . . for the sake of the thing that encompasses or transcends everything: liberation, satori, God, enlightenment."

William James describes religious conversion in *The Varieties of Religious Experience:* "To say that a person is 'converted' means . . . that religious ideas, previously peripheral in his consciousness, now take a central place, and that religious aims form the habitual center of his energy." He goes on to say that religious experience should be "judged by its fruits not its roots." In other words, we know our religion has meaning when it increases our loving-kindness and integrity. The specific beliefs or their historicity are not as important as what they lead us to do and be.

In the Christian view, just as conversion would be impossible without grace, so would unconditional altruism. Thus, grace is what makes it possible for us to love in an untiringly forgiving way. Saint Paul also sees good deeds as fruits of grace at work: "By the grace of God I am what I am, and his grace in me is not without effect. . . . I worked . . . yet it was not I but the grace of God that is in me" (1 Cor. 15:10).

Saint Paul likewise shows how grace is transcendent, beyond ego agency: "Now to the Spirit who, by the power at work within us, is able to accomplish abundantly far more than anything we can ask for or imagine" (Eph. 3:20). To remain in the state of grace is thus itself a grace.

The religious rituals we engage in meaningfully are examples of the means of grace. This does not mean they magically produce grace, only that they place us in a position in which grace can come through to us. Nor is grace a metaphysical reality or spiritual commodity. It is an opening of our potential for love and for virtuous living.

Patriarchy and Limits

A Catholic theological distinction is made between two types of grace: Actual grace happens in any here-and-now experience and is meant to lead us to God. Sanctifying grace is the life of God in us, what readies us for heaven, which comes to us mainly through the sacraments. From Martin Luther's Protestant perspective, grace is granted on the basis of faith alone, not because of rituals we engage in or even because of good works that we perform—though both contribute to pious living.

We cannot overlook the correlation between insistence on a limited access to grace—from rituals performed by legitimately ordained ministers—and the maintenance of patriarchal authority. As long as God is male only and wholly other than nature or ourselves, it will take official channels to reach him. We do not then have personal access to grace but are assured of it only by allegiance to a church and obedience to its commands.

Limiting the availability of grace and parceling it out to those whom the authorities deem worthy contradicts the nature of grace as free and beyond the control of any person or group. Some of the Gnostics of the early Christian centuries held that only a chosen few had access to truth. This perspective seems to endure in the understanding and exercise of patriarchal authority. The true grace given to those in authority is that of service. A re-visioning of hierarchy makes it about the grace of respectful collegiality with all believers.

Medieval scholastic theologians, with a patriarchal orientation, understood God's grace as something extrinsic to us, something poured into us from above through the institutional church—and only when we were properly disposed to it by adherence to official beliefs and respect for church authority. This is a danger in any patriarchal religion. Then grace is not perceived as freely given but as something earned by those in the true church who participate in its legitimate rituals.

In reality, grace transcends the entitlements of religion or individuals. The greatest grace can come to an atheist. Since grace is free, there is no correlation between grace and performance or belief.

A corollary to the limited understanding of grace is in the theological configuring of creation. In medieval theology, creation was seen as an act of God, who made something out of nothing. This is a dualistic perspective, wherein a God up there makes a world down here. In this view, God is above nature, not one with it. We can see how this belief literally de-natures our sense of grace.

In a more recent version of Christian theology, we find an alternative, far more liberating description: creation is ongoing rather than being something that has happened once and for all. This makes all creation a generous gift of God's ongoing love. Grace is divine favor in every moment and place, for all time, a reality ever in motion. God is not up there making it all out of nothing but is the divine-in-all continually cocreating all with our participation. In this nondual view, we are all cocreators when we further the spiritual aims of evolution—a world of justice, peace, and love. This is how grace makes the divine alive in us. This is how we remain in the state of grace.

The following two quotations powerfully express this mystical understanding:

> I saw Him in my house. Among all the everyday things He appeared unexpectedly and became utterly united and merged with me, and leaped over to me without anything in between, as fire to iron, as light to glass. And He made me like fire and like light. And I became that which I saw be-

fore and beheld from afar. I do not know how to relate this miracle to you. I am human by nature, and God by grace.
—SAINT SIMEON STYLITES THE YOUNGER (QUOTED BY
JOSEPH CAMPBELL IN *The Hero with a Thousand Faces*)

In that radiant awareness, every I becomes a God, every We becomes God's sincerest worship, and every It become God's most gracious temple.
—KEN WILBER, *A Brief History of Everything*

Two Helpful Images

In Catholic theology there are two doctrines that show how grace is part of our common human legacy: the Treasury of Merit and the Communion of Saints. We can treat them, as we can all doctrines, as archetypal metaphors. This maintains their importance and deep meaning without requiring us to take them literally. They can be acknowledged as deep realizations about the nature of our common humanity. Longstanding religious concepts can tell us something about who we are at a level that logical thought or linear literalism might overlook. This is why symbols in religion and myth show us the unimagined expanse of our being and purpose.

The Treasury of Merit refers to the accumulated merits gained for humanity from the life and sufferings of Christ and the early Christian martyrs. It is not that merits produce grace. The treasury concept implies that the graces given to others—Christ and the martyrs—can be transferred to us.

In medieval times, popes declared that they held the keys to the treasury; they could dispense merits in the form of indulgences based on donations. Luther accepted the Treasury of Merit idea but rebelled against authoritarian control over it—particularly the notion that the merits could be bought or sold, as with indulgences. The merits are available as graces to all people who act with goodwill. This points to an essential element in adult faith, the belief that grace is not in the hands of authority figures who dispense it to us if we follow their rules. It is a gift freely given by a source beyond human authority.

The Treasury of Merit is based on another belief, the Communion of Saints. This refers to a solidarity and generous interchange among all the members of the church, both past and present. Saint Paul wrote: "We, being many, are one body in Christ, and every one members one of another" (Rom. 12:5). The church in heaven, that is, the saints, intercedes with God and prays for those in purgatory and us on earth. The church on earth prays for those in purgatory and to the saints in heaven. Thus, the branches of the church care for each other and are conduits of grace to each other. Saint Thomas Aquinas, in *Quodlibet,* wrote: "All the saints intended that whatever they did or suffered for God's sake should be of value not only to themselves but to the whole Church." He is referring to the Communion of Saints, but he is also confirming the definition of love as continual caring connection—another description of the Communion of Saints.

This reminds us of the bodhisattva teaching in Buddhism, that some enlightened beings who have passed away keep helping those on earth today. Dogen Zenji, in *The Treasury of the True Dharma Eye,* wrote: "Beneficial action is an act of oneness, benefiting self and others together." We also note that the Tibetan Buddhist commentary by Geshe Kelsang Gyatso on the practice of offering to the spiritual guide, is coincidentally entitled *Great Treasury of Merit.* The ceremony of offering is performed twice a month in Kadampa Buddhist centers or at any time by individual practitioners. It is referred to as "the supreme gateway" to receiving blessings and graces in Tantric Mahamudra practice. We continue to notice that psychic realizations, especially about grace, are similar in a variety of traditions.

Regarding the two theological concepts, the Treasury of Merit and the Communion of Saints, we can now look at how to take them as metaphors that help us understand our collective human nature.

Jung described the collective unconscious as cosmic consciousness with a divine source. Coincidentally, he called the collective unconscious a *treasury* of wisdom and images that we share with all humankind. Our most valuable personal explorations, therefore, involve mining the images that strike us or that we meet in dreams. They contain openings to the graces waiting to come through to us.

Both the Treasury of Merit and the Communion of Saints imply that wisdom and love are not limited to any group or time. These graces are accessible to all of us from our ancestral past, our collective human heritage. The wisdom we can gain is not based on any library of human knowledge. It is available from a collective storehouse, a collective consciousness into which our ancestors have made abundant deposits. What we know today is and was, as Jung says, "immemorially known."

Every human has as her or his heritage what all previous humans have gained and been graced by. Wise and mighty companions have shared their powers with us. They did not want to keep their gifts to themselves. They stored them for the use and benefit of all of us. This shows our transhistorical connectedness as humans. It also shows that truly evolved beings care about the evolving of all beings. Not surprisingly, we see this even in pagan belief as reported by Plutarch in *De Genio Socratis:* "According to Hesiod, the souls delivered from birth are at rest and absolved. They become guardian spirits of humankind. . . . Like old athletes, they do not lose interest in us but show goodwill and sympathetic zeal to us still engaged in life, setting forth with us and shouting encouragement as they see us approach, and at last attain, our hoped-for goal."

In addition, in the teachings of the Treasury of Merit and the Communion of Saints, we learn something crucially important about the here and now. This *now* is not a naked isolated moment, hermetically sealed, but an entry into a coherent, shareable past. It is called a void only because it is void of concepts. Yet it is more compelling than any insight on any day. In truly meditative moments, we feel the plenitude that a moment can bring when it includes contact with our collective humanity. That gift dimension in every here and now is what makes it so vital in life and meditation. We rest in the here and now as the container of all graces.

Thus, there is no present moment only; every moment is beneficially linked to all the riches of prior times and is a prelude to what will come. This is reminiscent of the connections in the Communion of Saints.

The two doctrines also show us we are not stranded here on earth, not even for a minute. We are in contact with all other humans who have preceded us and who are on earth with us now. Every meditation practice of every person is benefiting all of us.

Saints and bodhisattvas, all of those who intend their spiritual practices for the good of others, show they care about our evolving journeys. They, both living and dead, want us to continue the tradition of growing in wisdom and compassion. They want us to join in their work of helping humanity grow and thrive. We draw from their repository of assets and add our own for the benefit of those here now and those who will come after us.

Dag Hammarskjöld, in his *Markings*, wrote: "Through me there flashes this vision of a magnetic field in the soul, created in a timeless present by unknown multitudes . . . whose words and actions are a timeless prayer: the Communion of Saints and within it an eternal life." Hammarskjöld's word *timeless* reminds us that the communion does not refer only to the past and how it enters the present. The exchange crosses the boundaries of past and future.

Indeed, a mature religious consciousness of an afterlife is not about a personal reward for work well done. It is an opportunity—read grace—to keep contributing to the welfare of humanity. This was expressed so tenderly by Saint Therese of Lisieux, a French saint of the nineteenth century: "I will spend my heaven doing good on earth."

The sense that humanity is a community that gains in order to share is an enduring truth in the perennial psychic wisdom of humanity. There is no heaven as reward, only heaven as more opportunity to love the world.

All we have explored in this section reminds us that we are continually sharing with one another in the ongoing enterprise of evolutionary progression on the human journey. We can perhaps rename the two beliefs now, in terms that have less cultural and doctrinal baggage, as the Treasury of Benefits and the Communion of Humanity.

Theological and mythic beliefs need not be taken literally, but neither are they to be dismissed. They have been conserving truths so profound that it takes centuries for their depth to be appreciated. They are like two matches struck felicitously in our contemporary darkness that flash a long-needed light.

> May the time come when humans, having been awakened to a sense of the close bond linking all the movements of this world, . . . shall be unable to give themselves to any one of their tasks without illuminating it with the clear vision that their work—however elementary it may be—is received and put to good use by a Center of the universe.
>
> —Pierre Teilhard de Chardin, *The Divine Milieu*

8

Grace in Buddhism

The gift of Dharma surpasses all gifts.
—DHAMMAPADA 354

There is no explicit teaching about grace in Buddhism. Grace is associated with theism, and Buddhism is nontheistic. Yet it would be a loss not to acknowledge a common human experience because of its association with theism. Along these lines, Stephen Batchelor, in *Living with the Devil,* says: "Whether myths we inherit from the past come from a monotheistic tradition such as Judaism or Christianity, or a non-theistic tradition such as Buddhism, they share the view that a human life is fully intelligible only as part of an immense cosmic drama that *transcends* it. Both believe *hidden powers* to be at work—whether of God or karma make little difference—that *have flung us* into this world to face the daunting task of redeeming ourselves for the remainder of eternity." I have italicized the references to the mythic and enigmatic cartography of grace. In that spirit, let's remind ourselves about what grace refers to as an archetype of assistance on our path. Then we can see how it shows up in Buddhism.

We remind ourselves that our understanding of grace in this book is of an uncaused and unexpected help, not based on merit, coming to us from beyond the egoic world.

In Buddhism no one has the power to summon up enlightenment at will, yet people have been enlightened. In fact, enlightenment is an ever-present option for any person. This is a way of saying that enlightenment is the fulfillment of our humanness, but our human efforts are not sufficient to get us there. To be fully human we need help. There is a saying in Buddhism: "Sometimes we turn the dharma wheel; sometimes the dharma wheel turns us." Sometimes we put in effective effort by our practices; sometimes our practice becomes what helps us, what becomes our support, our encouragement, our sustenance, our guide. This seems to point to the presence of grace as a requisite on the spiritual path.

In Buddhism things and beings have no independent existence but are dependent on conditions and causes. Karma, mentioned in the quotation above, is one of five types of causality, the five *niyama dhammas,* categories of natural law that continually interact in our changing world. So karma is not to be construed as the only explanation of why things happen. Here are the five causes and conditions that seem to account for reality as we know it. The fifth one seems to point to the subject of grace.

Karma-niyama refers to how actions produce consequences.

Utu-niyama refers to nature, the physical universe and its laws.

Bija-niyama is the biological world, especially with respect to seeds and growth: barley seeds will only produce barley; mammals act like mammals.

Citta-niyama refers to the impact of our mental processes, such as psychological states.

Dharma-niyama refers to the power of the dharma and of the help we receive from bodhisattvas. The root of the word *dharma* is *dhri,* Sanskrit for "hold." Dharma holds and upholds all that is and maintains it in harmony. (This sense of holding as both accompaniment and nurturance is what is implied in the experience of grace.)

Niyama also has a connection to grace in that help comes to us based not on our merits but on the compassion of enlightened beings toward us. In Buddhist terms, grace can then be understood as *dana,* generosity, to us from them.

Such grace makes for progress toward enlightenment, adding to what might be missing in our efforts. Compare the spaciousness in this view to the tightly determined fatalism that is often presented as karma when it is limited in meaning to an absolute correlation between what we do and what then happens to us. When karma is understood as the origin of all that happens, the element of grace is ignored and life becomes one-dimensional.

The thirteenth-century founder of the Soto school of Zen, Dogen Zenji, wrote in *The Treasury of the True Dharma Eye:* "Reality is a spiritual experience; nature is practicing Buddhism." This profound comment seems to indicate that reality and nature are perfectly in sync with spiritual consciousness. We can configure this concept in reverse: our spiritual practices show us what we can find in reality and in nature. Hence, when we show generosity—*dana*—that very act gives us an assurance that the universe is also generous to us. Our practices are thus correlated with graces. What we do is what we receive.

Resources on the Buddhist Path

The presence and action of grace can be glimpsed most clearly in three Buddhist teachings: in *bodhicitta;* in the three refuges; and in the help of teachers, ancestors, and bodhisattvas.

Bodhicitta, enlightened heart, as we saw in a previous chapter, is our movement toward the enlightened life and our commitment to share it with others—our impulse toward enlightenment as an important or primary focus. The instigating power that moves us in the direction of enlightenment is not caused by us. We do not give ourselves the incentive to embark on the path. It simply happens, suddenly or gradually— the two styles of grace. We do not make anything happen. We are given a chance, an opportunity to embrace the path of enlightenment. Shantideva expressed this is in *The Way of the Bodhisattva:*

> I am like a blind man who has found
> A precious gem inside a heap of dust.
> For so it is, by some strange chance,
> That bodhichitta has been born in me.

We can substitute the word *grace* for "chance" when we describe grace as meaningful chance.

When *bodhicitta* has been born in us, we also become interested in and then pledged to the bodhisattva path, that is, to bringing enlightenment to others. We cannot make this happen either. Indeed, the ego has no motivation to surrender itself for the good of others. Our enthusiasm about sharing the dharma in loving-kindness simply happens to us, which is just what is implied in the word *grace*—help that happens from beyond our ego, entitlement, or merit. Nonetheless, practices such as mindfulness and loving-kindness can help us open to bodhicitta. We continue to see, on all spiritual paths, how grace to us and effort by us felicitously combine.

Here is the final aspiration from the Tibetan sutra The Good Wish of Great Power: "May beings of the three spheres one and all by the prayer of my contemplation . . . finally attain Buddhahood." We also seek to become mediators of grace in the world, that is, bodhisattvas, enlightened beings who help others move toward the same light that they have found.

Buddhist Mahayana teaching distinguishes relative and absolute *bodhicitta:* Relative *bodhicitta* happens when the practitioner works for the benefit of all beings as equal to his own. Absolute, or ultimate, *bodhicitta* refers to the union of our awareness of emptiness and our acting with compassion. The awareness is the wisdom that sees all that is as empty of separate existence, as utterly connected. The practitioner who understands this is free from dualistic definitions of what the world is or should be. This is what makes compassion not a top-down practice but a lateral generosity, because it is based on an acknowledgment of human oneness. In addition, resting in emptiness is freedom from fear, since fear constricts our options and emptiness creates space for them.

The two styles go together. Without absolute *bodhicitta,* the relative might become maudlin. Without the absolute, the relative might become nihilistic, resulting in separation from others and lack of concern for their welfare.

Pema Chödrön, in *The Places That Scare You,* offers this view:

Bodhichitta exists on two levels. First there is unconditional bodhi-chitta, an immediate experience that is refreshingly free of concept, opinion, and our usual all-caught-upness. It's something hugely good that we are not able to pin down even slightly, like knowing at gut level that there's absolutely nothing to lose. Second there is rela-tive bodhichitta, our ability to keep our hearts and minds open to suffering without shutting down.

Absolute *bodhicitta* can also be understood as the love in our en-lightened nature that makes no distinction between lover and beloved. This is a permanent feature of our true nature. Relative *bodhicitta* re-fers to how we show the love within us, how we act lovingly. Endless love calls for endless loving. This takes daily practice.

We might say that absolute *bodhicitta* is inborn grace; relative *bo-dhicitta* applies it to relationships. We cultivate what grace has initi-ated. In this perspective, the relationship between absolute and relative *bodhicitta* is like the relationship between grace and effort. The grace of absolute *bodhicitta* is the container in which our intention to prac-tice love incubates and grows. Absolute *bodhicitta* is based on our in-eradicable inner goodness, the grace that is our true nature.

The Tibetan teacher Patrul Rinpoche proposes three levels of *bo-dhicitta* using archetypal images: The most fundamental level is the way of the king, who is out for himself but is aware of his need for a kingdom and subjects. The middle level is that of the ferryman, who wants to get his passengers across the river and in doing so is con-cerned to get himself across too. The highest level is that of the self-sacrificing shepherd, whose concern is for all of his sheep, so he will dare danger to himself for their safety.

The second trace of grace in Buddhism is in how it offers three ref-uges from craving, illusion, and fear. They are the three treasures avail-able to us on our spiritual path: the Buddha, the dharma, and the sangha. The Buddha is the historic Buddha, Siddhartha Gautama, who encourages us as an exemplar, a human who was indeed fully en-lightened. Ultimately the Buddha is our own enlightened mind. The dharma is the enlightened teaching. The sangha is the fellowship of practitioners on the enlightened path.

As we turn to these refuges, we notice that through them we have access to more power than can be accounted for by our own capacities or efforts. Something is magnifying our powers and supporting our endeavors. The Dalai Lama confirms and adds to this idea in his *Way to Freedom:* "The three jewels have the capacity to protect." He goes on to describe our trust in the capacity of the three refuges to protect us: "We develop this trust through meditating on the qualities of the Buddha, dharma, and sangha." Our follow-up practices are always key to the full flourishing of grace in our lives.

A third indicator of grace in Buddhism is our access to free assistance from teachers, ancestors, and the many bodhisattvas who have preceded us over the centuries. We are surrounded by broadcasters of the dharma and meditators in support of our practice. The Mind Ground Sutra in East Asian Buddhism refers to four graces: teachers, parents, the sovereign, and the three refuges.

We are also fortunate to have our present-day teachers helping us. To stay on the path is to continue in our practices of mindfulness and loving-kindness. The teacher is the external helper. He or she awakens our inner teacher, our own intuition and wisdom. The teacher and teachings give ongoing encouragement and make helpful corrections that keep us on the path.

We are also aided by ancestors. In his *Beyond Thinking,* Dogen Zenji refers to the power of what we can call grace: "Buddha ancestors, out of their kindness, have opened the wide gate of compassion in order to let all sentient beings enter realization. . . . Those who think Buddhas appear only in the human realm have not yet entered the inner chambers of Buddha ancestors. . . . Shakyamuni in the heavenly realm teaches in far more varied ways, in one thousand styles, in ten thousand gates."

Assistance from bodhisattvas is another indication of help to us on the path from beyond our own ego. Bodhisattvas are touched by our yearning for enlightenment and our practice of the teachings. They become assisting forces on the path. The bodhisattvas are personifications of grace-giving forces freely and generously serving us. In *The Way of the Bodhisattva,* Shantideva states:

And now to Mañjughosaha [Bodhisattva of Wisdom] I bow,
Whose kindness is the wellspring of my good intent.
And to my virtuous friends I also bow
Whose inspiration gave me strength to grow.

Buddhist sutras often invoke bodhisattvas to help us. In the bodhisattva precepts ceremony (*jukai*), initiates chant a verse that begins, "Om, *bodhisattva mahasattvas,* please concentrate your hearts on me." The initiates on the path are asking help from beyond themselves, from powers that exceed what any of their practices can produce. At the same time, in the *metta* practice, loving-kindness, we continue to aspire to become conduits of enlightenment to one another.

Finally, we notice that in the spectrum of Buddhist traditions, graces come through in ways besides the three mentioned above. For instance, the use of mantras and mudras (hand gestures) and the honoring of sacred images and objects also help us in moving toward enlightenment. In most mythic and religious traditions, graces come through to us from specially designed objects. In fairy tales, for instance, we notice the hero is aided by talismans, amulets, potions, magical objects. These are metaphors for archetypal assisting forces that arise from nature and take the form of symbolic actions and tangible things.

In Christian theology we find the term *sacramentals.* These are devotional objects or acts that help us stay on the path, for example, an icon, a rosary, a special prayer. In Buddhism the corresponding sacramentals would be the symbols or reminders of enlightenment, images of the Buddha, statues, mandalas, robes, bells, rituals, incense, candles, meditation cushions. All of these accoutrements of practice encourage us on the path and help focus us. They are graces in that they enact enlightened consciousness if we use and honor them to further our practice. They remind us that grace is mediated through people, places, and things.

To summarize what we have discussed so far, we can say that we know we did not make ourselves want enlightenment, so the first step onto the path, *bodhicitta,* is grace. We know we did not have it in us to stay with our practices with perseverance, so to the extent that we did, it was through the grace of encouragement. We know we were no match for the seductions of desire and attachment, so our freedom from them was the grace of protection and victory.

We moved from the foretaste of enlightenment to work toward enlightenment to letting go of all that stands in the way of it. And we remain aware that all three of these culminate in enlightenment, not as an object of attainment, but as a contact with what has always been true for us. It certainly takes grace to enter such an unusual awareness in minds as driven and chaotic as ours.

> Grace fills empty spaces; only entering where there is a void to receive it. And grace itself creates the void.
> —SIMONE WEIL, *Grace and Gravity*

The Pure Land Tradition

We can learn something about grace from the Pure Land tradition of Buddhism. Among the various traditions, it's the one that most specifically and unabashedly emphasizes blessings upon us, to a degree that it is resonant with the Western understanding of graces.

The Pure Land tradition is part of Mahayana Buddhism. Its emphasis is on devotion to Amitabha Buddha. The Pure Land sutras, composed in the second century, say that the bodhisattva Amitabha vowed to spend his life saving all sentient beings and giving them rebirth in the Western Paradise. This is the Pure Land that gives access to nirvana. It is pure in the sense of free from fear, desire, and the need for rebirth in the samsaric, that is, the cyclic karmic world of fear and craving. Our entrance into the Pure Land is assured if we say the name of Amitabha with trust in his powers of liberation, freely given, and the effectiveness of his commitment to help us. We thus rely on his vow as a resource in our practice, as a source of assistance—as Christians rely on the commitment of Christ to humanity. The reliance is surrender to a power beyond our own ego. Since the pronunciation and honoring of a name is not equivalent in power to the result, nirvana, we are meeting the characteristic element of grace: a gift that exceeds our practices and efforts.

We rely on the blessings, graces, of Amitabha that come to us unbidden and unconnected to merit. There is no cause/effect relationship, only gift and receptivity. The emphasis is on invocation and gratitude. We place our intention for enlightenment and engage diligently in the practices that foster it. Here too there is no cause/effect connection, only commitment to practice and trust in the long line of wise teachers who show us how to perform them.

A Pure Land devotee believes that Amitabha and other bodhisattvas will show themselves to him or her at the hour of death and carry the devotee to paradise.

We see some similarities and differences in religious and Buddhist approaches to grace: In Pure Land Buddhism, Amitabha transfers the grace he himself merited to the practitioner. This mirrors the Christian view in which Christ gives his merits to us as graces. Alternatively, in the monotheistic view of Judaism and Islam, grace flows from God's own life and loving-kindness. It is not the result of anyone's merits. Likewise, in the monotheistic view, grace comes from a single source, God. In Buddhism, grace is diffuse and comes from a variety of sources. Chapter 25 of the Lotus Sutra, for instance, speaks of salvation, grace, coming "from both human and non-human sources."

Power from Self, Power from Other

There is no specific word for grace in Sanskrit, but *adhisthana* comes the closest. It means blessing, spiritual power. Philologically it is "what is received by giving." This concept, reminiscent of the Western view of grace, appears both in the Mahayana and Vajrayana traditions of Buddhism. Unlike the teachings in Christian theology, the blessings, freely given benefits, derive not from a supreme being but from Buddha himself and the lineage of teachers who care about our liberation. Thus,

Chögyam Trungpa, in *The Profound Treasury of the Ocean of Dharma*, writes: "We speak . . . about the experience of blessing, *adhisthana*, and although we invoke all kinds of power and energy, those things do not come from some entity existing either within us or outside of us. . . . We do not start from anywhere. When we invoke deities there is no reference to a special [separate] existence." Pema Chödron states in the foreword to *It's Up to You* by Dzigar Kongtrül: "Somehow, both the depth of his studies and the lineage blessings of his teachers come through when he speaks." His studies are the effort; I interpret "the lineage blessings" as the graces. The lineage of teachers is the conduit of the blessing that comes from the dharma, the exalted wisdom that transcends ordinary intelligence.

The *adhisthana* of Buddha himself mediates for us the teachings of enlightened masters in the sutras. Thus, in the Tibetan version of the Heart Sutra, it is because of the Buddha's blessings that the bodhisattva Avalokiteshvara is able to teach the dharma. Avalokiteshvara is the bodhisattva of compassion, an emanation of Amitabha. The Dalai Lama is regarded by Tibetan Buddhists as an incarnation of Avalokiteshvara. This bodhisattva, like all of them, does not have a single incarnation but is believed to be appearing in manifold emanations at all times. This is certainly reminiscent of grace, here always and everywhere to assist us on the path.

The Buddha shared his teachings for more than forty years with a vigorous and convincing charisma. This was *adhisthana*, the generous empowerment that can come to all humans in some way.

The Lotus Sutra begins with a vision of the Buddha beaming white light from his third eye. It is powerful enough to illuminate the universe. This is a metaphorical way of showing the nature of enlightenment as gift rather than achievement. We bathe in Buddha's awakening and we are awakened.

In Tibetan, *adhisthana* is *jinlap*. The literal translation is "a wave of splendor" or "waves of grace." This seems to indicate that something unplanned by us is coming to us from the lineage of the enlightened masters. Devotion to the teachers opens the treasury of lineage blessings, essential to enlightenment and given freely.

The Buddhist scholar D. T. Suzuki says that *adhisthana* describes the transforming power of the Buddha: "The Buddha is creative life itself. He creates himself in innumerable forms with all the means native to him. This is called his *adhisthana,* as it were, emanating from his personality. The idea of *adhisthana* is one of the Mahayana landmarks in the history of Indian Buddhism and it is at the same time the beginning of the 'other-power' (*tariki* in Japanese) school as distinguished from the 'self-power' (*jiriki*), terms in Japanese Buddhism."

Tariki is power from another, as in the Pure Land tradition, in which our enlightenment depends on the graces given to us by Amitabha Buddha.

Jiriki is power from self, from our focused effort toward the enlightened life.

In Zen especially, we notice this accent on personal practices for reaching enlightenment. Yet Zen also relies on "other power" by giving importance to another, the *roshi,* the teacher who shows the way. Zen Buddhism also acknowledges other power in the teaching that when we practice *zazen* meditation, all things are practicing with us, so our practice is never merely our own. We recall the words of Shunryu Suzuki in *Not Always So:* "Although we practice with people, our goal is to practice with mountains and rivers, with trees and stones, with everything in the world, everything in the universe, and to find ourselves in this big cosmos.... [Then] we know intuitively [as a grace] which way to go."

Jiriki can't literally be from a self in any case, since there is no solid self in Buddhism. Thus, *tariki* and *jiriki* work together, confirming the fact of nonduality on the spiritual path.

We want to cross the river of samsara. The boat is *tariki,* what is given to us, and our rowing, what we do, is *jiriki,* but it too requires grace, since there is no separate self doing the rowing. Here is an example from a legend: Bodhidharma needed to cross the river but had no boat. He saw a reed and stepped on it as if it were a raft, and it carried him across. Bodhidarma understood that *tariki* and *jiriki* work together, so he trusted that the reed was there on the shore from another power and his faith-effort of trusting it was required as his own power. We notice again and again this combination of trust in grace and commitment to effort. It is how we make the transition from the arid shore of ego to the fertile shore of enlightenment.

To summarize, we can say that in Buddhism enlightenment is beyond human power to conjure but within human power to receive. We require a power that compensates for and enlarges our practices on our journey to enlightenment. This is a way of saying we can't get across the river of light on our own steam, but since we do somehow cross it anyway, there must be another force at work assisting us.

Indeed, we are already enlightened, through an inborn grace, but we can't control the time at which we become aware of it; we can't create that gift moment ourselves. That is the mysterious gift, ongoing and immediate, that is available to everyone at every moment. It is up to us to let it in through our ongoing practices and also our gratitude. This is letting the light through.

The Pali canon also offers a clue to what might be called help from a source transcendent of ego: "There is, oh monks, an unborn, an unbecome, an unmade, an uncompounded; if, oh monks, there were not here this unborn, unbecome, unmade, uncompounded, there would not here be an escape from the born, the become, the made, the compounded. But because there is an unborn, an unbecome, an unmade, an uncompounded, therefore there is an escape from the born, the become, the made, the compounded" (Udana VII 1–3).

In Buddhism there is no transcendent supreme being. There is no self to be enlightened, no others to save. Yet the passage above certainly shows a sense of the transcendent. This is grace understood as what helps us go beyond ego. Such a liberating possibility is the foundation of our confidence on the spiritual path.

Finally, Buddhism itself is *dana,* a generous grace to the world. It brings an incomparable wisdom and a way of life that cherishes and extends loving-kindness. And it does all of this without beliefs or institutional controls.

9

Grace in Nature

I only went out for a walk and finally concluded to stay out
till sundown, for going out, I found, was really going in.
— JOHN MUIR, *My First Summer in the Sierra*

We may seek relationship. We may yearn for a partner. We want to
fall in love with someone who will be with us always. What
about falling in love with nature, always and everywhere with us? Pierre
Teilhard de Chardin did this as a way of loving God. John Muir fell in
love with nature. Both thereby found the universe in their own hearts.

Graces are built into the natural order. The universe is granting benefits moment by moment. This planet with its sun, moon, stars, seasons, and ecosystem is a continuum of favor to us. Every sudden leap in
evolution is likewise a grace.

The natural world is beautiful not to please our sense of aesthetics
but because it generates, supports, and nurtures life, just what feminine energy does, just what grace does.

The fact of grace at work in the world implies that the universe is
friendly. This does not mean that the universe will reverse the law of
gravity when we fall off a bridge. A friendly universe does guarantee,
however, that its evolution is a continuous progression toward more

consciousness and more connectedness and that we are included in that thrilling arc.

Love of nature cannot have strings attached. It is not about how nature will come through for us. A true love of nature is love of the givens of the natural world, with all of its joys and dangers. Mother Nature may not calm the wind, but our yes to what is can calm us.

> Again and again I say that when we refer to Mother Earth, she is deserving of the name.
>
> —LUCRETIUS, *On the Nature of Things*

Flow and Field

Alfred North Whitehead proposed that the real world is not to be thought of as a collection of physical materials but as moments of experience. They flow together in ways that give us a singular sense of reality and of time. When we mistake the flow as something solid and fixed, we fall into what he calls "the fallacy of misplaced concreteness." His suggestion reminds us that our individual identity—like all that exists—is flow and change, not solidity and fixedness. Grace is also a flow. We see this in the continuous cycles of growth, decay, and rebirth—each a benefit in the web of life. Nature is showing us who we are and what to expect from a human life.

Grace is change, since it changes us. It is not something stationary at any moment, not something separate in any instant. Grace, like all that is, abides in connectedness. It is a relationship, not a thing. Every thing exists in concert with everything else. We are reminded of a statement attributed to Thomas Merton: "God is not somebody else." We also recall the Buddhist teaching that nothing has intrinsic existence; all is contingent, dependent, interconnected. Nothing exists in isolation; everything is thriving because it is relating.

Our theological sense of what grace is has changed with our awakening to the new universe paradigm. From this perspective grace is not only a special entrance of the divine into human life but an ongoing intention/action, the evolutionary momentum in all that happens. When we understand that physical realities are more like relationships than they are like solid mass, we can appreciate nature and ourselves as a lively and ever-expanding *field*. Quantum physics proposes that the whole world is a field of energy, that matter is simply slowed-down energy. In a field, such as a field of gravity or a magnetic field, the whole supersedes any of the parts but needs all the parts. Field energy is indeterminate but always generative. This is analogous to grace. It too is a moving, working, energizing, catalyzing element, and also one over which we have no control. We recall a biblical reference to that effect: "The Spirit blows where it will" (John 3:8). The freely moving, gift dimension of nature. Indeed, we might go so far as to ask: Was grace all along the spiritual name of what we have called the life force of the universe?

Spiritual usually refers to the transcendent, that which is more than what meets the eye, beyond our ordinary perception. Yet as we have been seeing, the transcendent is also *in* all that meets the eye. Nature—and we—are the ways the transcendent becomes immanent. So what we refer to as transcendent resides in living things. The transcendent is immanent in all that is. The transcendent and the immanent coalesce in the evolving universe. Thus, nature helps us see that the transcendent is not the opposite of the immanent. They are two aspects of one reality—the one reality in all the universe.

It is the style of nature and of the evolutionary process to be continually transcending itself. Our entire arc of existence is fervently bent in that spiritually alive and fiery direction. Thus, grace can be appreciated as a driving force of evolution.

Sudden unexplained advances in evolution seem to be examples of forces in nature that assist in the development of our planet and its species. Progress does not have to be limited, then, to the survival of the fittest. As complex systems organize themselves, new levels of patterning and new properties arise, for example, in the move from inert matter to life to consciousness. These are examples of leaps in the process of evolution. They certainly grant an inkling of grace at work.

Pierre Teilhard de Chardin wrote in *Forma Christi:* "Grace does not force us to enter another universe; it introduces us into an extension of our own universe." Thus, grace can be considered deeply material, deeply natural, deeply human. As long as grace is tied to a supernatural otherworld, we are caught in division and thereby miss our chance to don the coat of many colors that it is.

In the Basilica of Saint Francis in Assisi there is a statue called *Saint Francis Honoring the Holy Spirit.* The saint is looking down at the earth to contact the Holy Spirit instead of looking up into the sky as we might expect. He seems to be reflecting the mystical realization of a later Franciscan, Saint Bonaventure, who wrote in *Collations:* "The gifts of the Holy Spirit are in all things." These religious concepts have preserved a consciousness of grace in nature that we are now ready to acknowledge. The only faith required is a passionate trust in the universe.

Time and Space

> The events in our lives happen in a sequence in time, but in their significance to ourselves they find their own order, a timetable not necessarily—perhaps not possibly—chrono-logical. The time as we know it subjectively . . . is the continuous thread of revelation.
>
> —EUDORA WELTY, *One Writer's Beginnings*

Grace appears continually in nature's play as two main characters: time and space.

Our ordinary experience of *space* is simply location, the place where we are, have been, or are going to. But sometimes a place has a charge or aura, imparts a feeling, seems to have a significance beyond what we see. For example, our original family home takes on special significance because of the important things that happened to us there. The space is singular in its power to move us. It seems to exist in a realm beyond an address, what is called a *temenos,* a sacred space. Then it feels like the center of the world, at least of our world.

Shrines and special historic or religious places have this same numinous aura. This is why pilgrimages have always been part of spiritual practice. We also notice that on a pilgrimage the gift of grace does not occur only upon arrival at the shrine. The conscious and deepening intention of the pilgrim already begins endowing the person with the healing graces she or he is seeking on every step of the way. We participate in the release of grace by our opening to it.

Sacred *time* is not like ordinary time, which, in our subjective experience, whizzes by or slows to a snail's pace. It is not sequential. Sacred time stands rather than passes. It is not consecutive but coincident. We lose any sense of consecutive minutes. It all feels like a single moment, a rich "now." There is no sense of the past as a day or a decade ago. Yet we can feel transported into the distant past at an event like a Passover meal that nonetheless is occurring in the present.

The transcendent dimension of place is infinity, of time is eternity. The main access to the eternal in time is presence in the now. In fact, full and deep abiding in the now is what is meant by eternity. Eternity might be seen as an entrance into and an abiding in the moment. When we enter the moment, it can feel like the clocks have stopped ticking and we have stepped out of the procession of minutes and hours. These transcendent moments recall what Jung called the numinous, what Abraham Maslow called peak experiences, what mystics called the sense of human-divine oneness.

In such epiphanies of the eternal, there is no sense of the future as an hour from now but a sense of a richly present entry into what the world is becoming or was always meant to be. Sacred time shows that eternity is not in the by-and-by but is the depth reality of this moment. This is the gift dimension of time.

When we experience eternity, we are no longer under the spell of a three-decker system of past, present, and future. We then realize that we live in time *and* beyond it, something we could never have found using only the tools of mind and ego. It took the grace in our true nature to reveal the paradox of the temporal and the eternal all in one. William Wordsworth described it in *The Prelude* as "something evermore about to be."

Our openness to grace prepares us to see into the transcendent not only in time but in everything that happens. The joy we feel at the birth of a child, the awe we feel in a forest, the ecstasy in an erotic connection, all reveal the transcendent. It is too often eclipsed, however, by our attachment to concepts or our fear of surprises.

Grace is related to time also in the experience of *timing*. The fact that time heals makes it a grace, since it is a benefit to us but not caused or controlled by us. Time in this instance is a manifestation of grace in that it is mysteriously untying a problematic knot or healing a wound for us. Every one of us has noticed that time makes a difference in our resolving old hurts or mistakes. We can acknowledge the gift dimension of time, the grace of natural suturing, without the need for our bringing the stitching tools. *Time heals* means grace heals in time.

Timing is important in the journey to enlightenment. Its moment is beyond our control. Timing has to be respected when it comes to inspiration, seeing the light, changing an attitude, awakening to a truth that was there all along but we were not ready to know it. We can appreciate a metaphor for timing in religious traditions: It took forty years for the Israelites to reach the Promised Land. In the Gospel account of Pentecost it took fifty days after Easter before the Holy Spirit came to enlighten and empower the apostles.

The ancient Greeks had two concepts of time. *Chronos* referred to ordinary sequential time. *Kairos* referred to a crucial moment, the right time for something significant to happen. *Kairos* is one chance only, and it is up to us to seize the opportunity, the grace, it offers. The Sophists emphasized the importance of change and circumstance. For them, we are spiritually mature when we remain on tap for the special moment in which we might receive an offer to move closer to our destiny. We find a resonant teaching in the New Testament in which the same word, *kairos,* is used to refer to the graced moment in which we fulfill our destiny: "the appointed time [*kairos*] in the purpose of God" (Mark 1:15).

In his book *The Interpretation of History,* the theologian Paul Tillich uses the word *kairos* to refer to crises that have arisen throughout history that summon us to take action. Thus the *kairos* is how time shows the arrival of a favorable circumstance for us to engage, take a step, make a commitment. As we saw above, since the invitation of grace respects our freedom, we can either say yes to that grace and step up to the plate or we can let the moment pass us by.

The *kairos* is sometimes momentary. An opportunity comes along, and we have only that instant to go with it. If we do, we spring forward; if we do not, we fall back. We see this idea in these challenge-laced lines from Shakespeare's *Julius Caesar:*

> There is a tide in the affairs of men
> Which, taken at the flood, leads on to fortune;
> Omitted, all the voyage of their life
> Is bound in shallows and in miseries.
> On such a full sea are we now afloat,
> And we must take the current when it serves,
> Or lose our ventures.

Comfort in Nature

On the personal level, we sometimes turn to nature for consolation or strength. We see an example of this in the poem "Snow-flakes" by Henry Wadsworth Longfellow:

> This is the secret of despair,
>   Long in its cloudy bosom hoarded,
>   Now whispered and revealed
>   To wood and field.

The poet can share with woods and fields the despair and sadness he has held inside himself. He feels that nature is open to this, welcoming his sorrow. Nature seems to be a healing force because it can receive his burden from him, hold it with him, and lighten it for him—the three dimensions of healing. Nature grants purchase to the zone of grace.

In Shakespeare's *Romeo and Juliet,* Juliet also wonders about grace from nature. She seems naive, but she is actually profoundly aware of deep spiritual powers in the universe: "Is there no pity sitting in the clouds, / That sees into the bottom of my grief?"

Juliet imagines that the same power we might describe as God "sitting" on his throne "in the clouds" is to be found and addressed in nature. This reflects our collective human realization that nature has a healing power, a grace we can sometimes access. It is far-reaching; it "sees into the bottom" of our story, our feelings, our destiny. It is no wonder that people have associated nature with the divine.

While pondering the quotation from Shakespeare, I was reminded of Michelangelo's *Pietà,* the archetypal image of a sorrowing mother holding her dead son. In that image, Mary can be seen to stand for Mother Nature. She also sits in a way that simultaneously shows compassion and grief, just the combination Juliet refers to.

In the *Pietà* we meet the archetype of compassion that sits still in grief, that feels it all the way to "the bottom," to use Juliet's words. We find a model of what it means to grieve while feeling loving-kindness at the same time. The *Pietà* shows us how to accept the unacceptable. We also come to understand an essential feature of compassion: We cannot feel compassion, sympathetic caring for another's pain, unless we are willing to feel our own pain. Compassion is lateral, from pain to pain, not top-down, from avoidance of one's own pain to awareness of another's.

In the full experience of someone's sadness, a compassion arises for similar griefs that others carry. We see this connection in Shakespeare's *King Lear:*

A most poor man, made tame to fortune's blows,
Who by the art of known and feeling sorrows
Am pregnant to good pity.

Thus, through the centuries, people—and we today—who gaze at the *Pietà* have felt that the Mother of Sorrows feels compassion for *us* in our sorrows, the consolation Juliet yearned for. We feel held by the Earth Mother as Christ is held in Mary's arms. We feel held by Mother

Nature in the same way. Our fascination with this archetype endures because we hanker to be held in the unconditional way we experience in Michelangelo's glorious work.

As an aside, we can go on to notice that graces come to us in individually tailored ways. They are free, so they are not parceled out equally or evenly. Each person has his or her own story. Demeter felt the need to retaliate because her daughter, Persephone, kidnapped into the underworld, was fated to have a darker story than she wanted for her. This is an archetypal way of alerting us parents to the fact that our children have to have their own story, no matter how far it strays from what we wanted for them. This is surely implied in the *Pietà,* in which Mary, unlike Demeter, holds Christ and his tortured destiny with grief but without judgment or a plan for retaliation.

Finally, the archetypal power of the image can strike us with an uneasy feeling, since it depicts Mother Earth in mourning, and we can feel that our sad record with maintaining the environment is implicated in her sadness.

Our Natural-Spiritual Challenge

> The divine is the enfolding of the universe, and the universe is the unfolding of the divine.
>
> —NICHOLAS OF CUSA, *On the Pursuit of Wisdom*

Spirituality today ranges from the superficial New Age focus on magic to a deep embrace of the power of myth and mysticism. Both of these extremes can turn into retreats from the world and its needs. A spirituality that truly works for our time has to be about passion for and commitment to the safety and evolution of the world and of each other. Such a spiritual practice will naturally include active participation in global ecological change. We take our places in the new spiritual arena not with the spectators but with those who are redesigning the world for justice, peace, and love. We can always trust that a mothering energy somehow supports us in that spiritual venture.

We can also journey deeply into a reverent, receptive awareness in which we find unique new ways to promote the evolution of our planet. We are energized, pushed, sent out to carry the message of love for the earth by awakening to the mandate to treat all creation with courtesy and care. Graces emerge that help us let go of greed and abuse of nature and make respect the invariable bottom line of all of our choices.

All love, including our love of nature, is motivated by a need for union, a desire to avoid separation. Thus, our interior spiritual journey does not keep us stuck in ourselves. Instead, we become more conscious of the world around us, its griefs and its longings. We find ourselves more aware of the needs of the planet and of how we can contribute helpful resources. This ignites a new fire, the sacred heart of spirituality, that burns with longing to preserve and nurture every living thing. Along these lines, the Jewish philosopher Martin Buber wrote in *Ecstatic Confessions:* "Whether the soul meets a loved human being or a wild landscape of heaped-up stones—from this human being, this heap of stones, grace catches fire and the soul . . . experiences the unity of 'I' and world."

Love for the earth happens only when we have a sense of oneness with nature. When we are in love, our heightened feeling state makes three realities, ordinarily separate, become one. The lover, the beloved, and the love between us feel like a single experience. The experience of being in nature and feeling one with it is in this same category. When we look *at* a tree, we do not fully see it yet. We see when "I to it" has turned to "only this." I recall once being alone in the woods and suddenly becoming aware of the powerful trees around me but not seeing them as separate from me, rather as the same as me. I said aloud, spontaneously and without planning or thinking: "I am what you are, transitory and everlasting."

I have noticed also in moments of true connection in therapy that the distinction between therapist, client, and the therapeutic work fades away. Those moments—in love, in nature, in therapy, or anywhere—are how we know that something real is happening. The real is that which is free of barriers, divisions, and rank.

The same model holds for grace. On an experiential level, the source, the recipient, and the grace itself feel like one and the same reality. To say, "Here and now I have a profoundly felt sense that grace is happening" indicates the deep unity that underlies and supports our life on the planet. This unity is not momentary but abiding, since grace is happening in every moment, though we feel it palpably only at special times. Such times are graces in themselves. Nature keeps presenting us with those times.

> Nature's secret process is to reveal essential being through the manifestation of its powers and forms. . . . To become ourselves is the one thing to be done; but the true ourselves is that which is within, our divine being. . . . It is by growing within . . . that we arrive at the creation of a world which shall be the true environment of divine living. This is the final object that nature has set before us. . . . To be and to be fully is nature's aim in us.
>
> —SRI AUROBINDO, *The Life Divine*

10

The Graces in Ourselves

Truth is within ourselves; it takes no rise
From outward things, ...
There is an inmost center in us all,
Where truth abides in fullness; ...
... and to know
Rather consists in opening out a way
Whence the imprisoned splendor may escape,
Than in effecting entry for a light
Supposed to be without.
                    —ROBERT BROWNING, *Paracelsus*

We humans are sometimes in touch with our wholeness and sometimes with our fragmentation. Both of these can be conduits of grace. We begin this chapter with a look at the grace in human wholeness. In the next section we consider the alternative of grace in fragmentation.

The true nature within us is a wholeness beyond what ego can craft or cancel. This transcendent wholeness is what makes any of our positive qualities more than they ordinarily would be. We can act from ego or from our true nature, the *more* than ego within us, the farthest reach of our humanness. For instance, the ego in us limits love to those who please us. In our true nature, our higher-than-ego self, our love is un-limited and unconditional. Thus we, in effect, grace ourselves when we show love in an unconditional way. It is a grace moment because we are tapping into the transcendent source inside us. That source made it possible for us to stretch into a vaster proportion of love than the cau-tions of ego would permit.

Our spiritual practices have as their purpose to release these vaster pos-sibilities in us. For instance, the practice of loving-kindness helps us love all beings, not just our near and dear, which is as far as the ego usually extends.

Mindfulness practice grants us a wisdom beyond the knowledge possible to our intellect. In any spiritual practice or endeavor, we are in contact with the *more* than we imagined possible. For instance:

- We can't see the value of humility without a shift in focus away from ego. That shift is a grace.
- We can't show unconditional love to everyone we meet without an opening of our heart in a more than ordinary way. That opening is a grace.
- In the mystical realm, we can't see the unity of all that is or the divine in all that happens without an interior swing into a new realization. That vision is a grace.
- In the realm of spirituality, we can't simply grasp that Bud-dhism or religion offers a way of life that matters. We can't make *bodhicitta* flourish in ourselves so that we are no longer concerned only with our own enlightenment but with that of others too. Something beyond ourselves has to turn us in that direction. That being turned is a grace.
- We can't just become activists working for peace in ways that put our comfortable lives at risk. The Jesuit pacifist John Dear, for instance, in his statement at his trial in 2008, declared: "It's a great grace to be in trouble with the empire for practicing nonviolence, for daring to offer a word of peace, for serving the God of peace." Taking that stand comes as a grace.
- We do not automatically embrace the teachings in the Sermon on the Mount: we love not only friends but enemies; we

do good to those who hate us rather than hurt them back. Love like that is a grace.

The references above are to the spiritual life. We often restrict our belief in the workings of grace to momentous spiritual conversions, special benefits, and major transformations. Grace, as the gift dimension of life, however, is active in all areas of our personal development. Thus, even beginning to do our psychological work takes a motivating force we cannot conjure. We cannot will such massive, often ego-demolishing changes. A force is at work, a higher power than ego. This is another way of seeing that our psychology and spirituality are inextricably linked—like everything in the universe. So much attention in recent years has been given to integrating the psychological and the spiritual. Grace is the link.

We return to our distinction between graces and grace. Graces come to us through people and experiences in the course of life. They show us where our work is, what is incomplete, what has become unsound. They show us healing possibilities in therapy, in programs, and in people who help us cultivate the best in ourselves and our relationships.

In addition we have an ongoing grace within ourselves, in the inner design of wholeness in our psyche, enduring no matter what happened to us in childhood or adulthood. We have an organismic drive toward health, a natural instinct for living in accord with our inner wholeness. This is grace built into our very nature. Here are five expressions of this from both psychological and spiritual sources:

> There is in us an innate given, a thrust toward individuation, which seems to continue during the entire life cycle.
>
> —MARGARET MAHLER

> There is in the psyche a process that seeks its own goal no matter what the external factors may be . . . the almost irresistible compulsion and urge to become what one is.
>
> —CARL JUNG

An inner wholeness presses its still unfulfilled claims upon us.

—EMMA JUNG

The work of works for humans is to establish, in and by means of each of us, an absolutely original center in which the universe reflects itself in a unique and inimitable way.

—PIERRE TEILHARD DE CHARDIN

The capacity for positive transformation lies naturally within the constitution of the mind itself.

—DALAI LAMA

Finally, recent brain research also makes the same point the Dalai Lama makes. Neuroplasticity refers to the brain's ability to alter our original conditioning so that we can function more effectively. Thus, there is something in us, an innate inclination, that *wants* us to activate our wholeness.

The Gift in Our Inadequacies

My imperfections and failures are as much a blessing as my successes and talents.

—MAHATMA GANDHI, *Harijan*

There is an urge in every person to "convert . . . gyves [fetters or shackles] to graces," as Hamlet says. We have an irrepressible inclination to release ourselves from the shackles of our inhibition and fear so we can find the graces residing in and beyond them. This happens when, by openness, we transcend the ego's one-sided focus on effort.

Our relentless pursuit of self-improvement, even of perfection, can blind us to the necessary role of grace in our development. Our self-acceptance, our becoming comfortable with ourselves just as we are, is a powerful way to open ourselves to grace. It's a way of acknowledging the gift dimension of our true nature, always here and already perfect. This inherent perfection does not mean that our personality does not need improvement. We continue to put effort into that lifelong project. But with a trust in the grace that thrives in deficiency, we can expend our effort in serene and wholesome ways. With an understanding of grace, our exertions do not feel compulsive, stressful, insistent on immediate results. We notice we are committed to working on ourselves but in a gentle, patient way. In other words, we are showing loving-kindness toward ourselves as we do our work. Thus, we engage in no self-recrimination, no self-scourging. We are not continually putting ourselves down for not doing enough. We are trusting that who we are, as we are, is just the right place for us to be. We have found the state of mind in which openness can best happen.

We accept our limitations because we trust our inner abiding wholeness, our enlightened buddha nature. We recognize it as our deepest reality, which cannot be eradicated by any personality discrepancy. Our goal is to trust in and manifest this, our true nature, with its enduring love, wisdom, and healing. Such full self-acceptance is itself an openness to grace—since our true nature is the best grace we have ever received.

Self-acceptance honors our ineradicable goodness and convinces us that every experience can be friendly toward us. It allows us to see a gift dimension not only in our virtues but in our inadequacies as well. Indeed, grace can appear when hope itself has abandoned us.

Since each of us is imperfect in some way, our imperfections connect us to one another. This is what makes compassion and love—the two shining graces of spiritual consciousness—possible.

In his essay "Compensation" Ralph Waldo Emerson wrote: "There is a crack in everything God has made." None of us is perfectly integrated, nor will we ever be. But that is irrelevant to the action of grace. Grace is not stymied or stopped by any of our misdeeds or deficits. Like love itself, grace keeps no record of wrongs. It is not based on how good we are or how often we have failed or fallen. An anonymous fourteenth-century English mystic wrote in *The Cloud of Unknowing:* "Grace is not given because of innocence or withheld because of guilt." Grace thus changes our concept of what is "deserved," since it transcends that ego concern. Indeed, the fact that grace comes to all affirms that all of us have transcendent worth. There is no one without the capacity for grace; no crimes or defects can obliterate it. No one can be excommunicated from grace. In fact, in keeping with the spiritual nature of paradox, grace is more likely to come through when there is room for it precisely because of cracks, blemishes, and flaws—openings, after all. Everything, including us, is in some way imperfect, damaged, fragmented. Yet that is a precise experience of our true nature: the paradox of incompleteness in wholeness. What supreme and optimistic news this is for beings as tattered, fractured, and bedraggled as we sometimes are. But as we discussed above, grace thrives in an atmosphere of imperfection. So we don't have to be afraid.

Grace is thus an alchemical experience, transforming what seems least valuable into what is most valuable. Our lead-weight shortcomings turn into the fine gold of spiritual progress. This is the paradoxical mystery of our humanity. Grace happens in the mud, not in the marble; in the tatters, not in the robes; in the empty bowl, not at the banquet table. This mystery of grace and human imperfection is expressed again by Ralph Waldo Emerson in his poem "Voluntaries": "So nigh is grandeur unto our dust."

Our own imperfections and shortcomings are a path to awakening us to our wholeness. This happens when we accept them but refuse to be stopped by them. They help us recognize grace at work in our lives. They show us answers to questions like these that I have asked myself:

Considering my childhood background, how did I become as sane as I am?

Having made so many foolish choices, how do I explain having as good a life as I have?

Given my story, how have I gained this amount of wisdom and accomplished as much as I have?

How did I get here from there?
I know help came from somewhere beyond this ego of mine.

In the poem "Love" by George Herbert, the poet is offered grace from Love, but he feels unworthy to receive it. He lists his faults, his inadequacies. He makes protestations of how undeserving of love he is:

> Love bade me welcome: yet my soul drew back,
>   Guilty of dust and sin.
> . . . .
> You must sit down, says Love, and taste my meat.
>   So I did sit and eat.

The inadequacies the poet sees in himself do not matter to Love. It still wants to give itself, and the poet accepts the gift.

Love does not give up on seeking connection with the poet. All it will take for him to experience the grace of being loved is a willingness to receive it: "I did sit and eat." This line is a reference to Revelation 3:20: "Behold, I stand at the door, and knock: If anyone hear my voice, and open the door, I will come in to him, and will sup with him, and he with me." Here we have a touching metaphor for how grace does not have to be sought out. It seeks us out and asks only that we open the door to let it in. Again we notice the theme of opening, making room, all it takes for grace to find us.

We see the same theme in this letter of Emily Dickinson's to Thomas Higginson: "Do not try to be saved—but let redemption find you—as it certainly will. Love is its own rescue, for we, at our supremest, are but its trembling emblems." Redemption is the grace of love gathering all in, both all that is in each of us and all of us in the human community. The fact that grace seeks us is the foundation of our hope—and joy.

Hopelessness is the belief that we are all there is, that everything depends on our own exertions—the essence of an atheistic perspective. Despair is the denial of grace. It is the illusion of separateness that disconnects us from the resources of grace always and everywhere knocking at our door.

There is dependable hope in the fact that we are being helped in our personal and global evolution by forces around and in us. Our inadequacies are being bolstered to supplement our move toward personal fulfillment. Our deficiencies are being outfitted for contributing to the evolution of the planet.

According to the Mahamudra Buddhist teachings, when it comes to the attaining of wisdom, our very confusion is as useful as our clarity. This is because *all* of our thoughts and experiences issue from and give us information about the true nature of our mind. Our presence and surrender to that wisdom is the very definition of enlightenment. Indeed, confusion can be understood as the grace of pressure upon our minds that moves us toward greater creativity and clarity. We keep noticing that grace always comes with a power to move us. We have heard the expression "Let go and move on." Grace makes both of those possible for us.

Finally, we can notice that power through deficiency is not limited to the recipient of grace. In most stories, the assisting forces that help the hero/recipient are somehow themselves wounded or damaged. For instance, in *The Wizard of Oz*, Dorothy is not assisted by three strapping rugby players or three samurai but by marginal vulnerable characters with missing parts. This is a metaphor for grace, since the help Dorothy receives is not from those with power but *through* those who are deficient or weak. This makes it clear that it is grace, transcendent help, that is really guiding things.

We see the same archetype at work in a more modern mythic story, the *Star Wars* trilogy: Luke can become a Jedi knight only by the aid of the least likely character, Yoda. Yoda is no Hercules, but he knows the path and how to traverse it.

More Than Self-Help

> Sometimes it happens that we receive the power to say yes to ourselves, that peace enters into us and makes us whole, that self-hate and self-contempt disappear, and then our self is reunited with itself. Then we can say that grace has come upon us.
>
> —PAUL TILLICH, *The Shaking of the Foundations*

There is no purely psychological change; the 12-step programs have shown us that by their accent on reliance on a higher power than ego. The spiritual life begins for us when we transcend and dispel our belief that anything depends entirely on ourselves. That is an attachment to the arrogant ego, an obstacle to any transformation.

Sigmund Freud said that psychological health was "the ability to love and work." This is a description of the minimum requirements for us to have a healthy ego. As we saw above, grace transcends ego so it can supplement our work. We can *love*, but by grace our love can go beyond those near and dear to us. Our *work* opens from career objectives and financial gain into service of others and of the planet. In both love and work, we can transcend the minimum standards attainable by psychological exertion. Such a happening in us is a grace.

As we saw earlier, in the Buddhist practice of loving-kindness, we begin by directing love to ourselves, then to those we care about, then to those to whom we are indifferent, then to those with whom we have difficulties, and finally, to all beings. Using this practice as a model, we can see that a wholesome ego can get us just far enough to be able to love ourselves and those we care about. But we need grace to love neutral persons, enemies, and unknown people everywhere. Grace is what exceeds the skill set of the healthy ego. We move then from minimal health to magnificent enrichment.

A psychological change, using the skills of a healthy ego, is a move from stuckness or dysfunctional behavior to behavior that leads to growth. Such growth can take forms such as these:

- We become more assertive when we have previously been passive.
- We are more apt to address rather than to deny our problems.
- We process what happens to us, understanding how it impacts us and others, rather than going through things unconsciously, inattentive to feelings, metaphors, and meanings.
- We learn conflict-resolution skills. We work toward resolving issues with others rather than letting them smolder into resentments.

- We become better able to handle the jolts of life with resilience, goodwill, and humor.
- In relating to others, we catch ourselves when our ego becomes inflated and entitled, finding ways to be cooperative and open instead.
- We have the skills needed to deal with guilt and fear.
- We express our feelings openly and noninvasively.
- We are open to the feelings of others.
- Our relationships become important enough to work on, and we are committed to doing so.

Each of these states can be acquired by practice. Each results in a healthier personality. This psychological change is the result of what we have achieved. It can be made to happen by our commitment to new health habits and better mental hygiene.

It is also true that with our new understanding of the neuroplasticity of the brain, we can expand many of our capacities and exceed the limits of our ingrained habits. Neuroplasticity is the ability of neurons to be altered by new experiences, attitudes, and practices. Thus, the force of will and practice can lay down new neural pathways. Remarkable changes, even transformations, seem to result from effort alone. The grace dimension remains, however, since neuroplasticity itself offers us a potential channel of grace.

How Transformation Happens

Grace always offers us more than we expect. Thus, grace takes us beyond the narrow distinction between functional and dysfunctional ego into the larger possibilities of personal change. For instance, psychologically, grace motivates us to cooperate with others rather than compete with them. If we have a conflict with someone, we might notice that we suddenly drop the need for revenge. We seek to create reconciliation with the other instead. We know this is out of character for us; we wonder where it came from, but we go with it. We like ourselves more this way. The fact is, whenever we notice that we like ourselves more, we can suspect that grace is at work. Grace is always about the *more* than ego thought of or dared to go for.

Since life is grace upon grace, our newfound loving consciousness may naturally expand our sense of community with all humans. We might find ourselves looking for ways to create reconciliation rather than retribution in the world at large. We not only want peace among our fellows but we want a *world* of justice, peace, and love.

A change in behavior is certainly possible without grace. For instance, right now I can choose not to have a cocktail but to stay focused on writing this chapter. I am doing this, or at least so it seems, by choice and willpower. Grace transcends willpower, so it is not about modification or adjustment of behavior. It is about transformation, a deeper level of change with a rich set of results.

Again and again as a therapist I have trusted that a client who has made progress has tapped into inner resources for healing that far outreach my skill. We do not often acknowledge the role or necessity of grace in psychological healing. Speaking of his wife, Shakespeare's Macbeth notices: "More needs she the divine than the physician." That "more" is the spiritual dimension, the grace that is essential in a healing process.

Here is a chart that summarizes what we have been describing in this chapter. It shows how the *more* can appear in some specific instances.

How Far the Ego Can Go	*Where the Self Can Take Us*
Love those near and dear	Love all beings
Be wise in our dealings with others	Tap into the perennial wisdom of humanity
Address our psychological issues	Heal our wounds and help others do the same
Deal with our fears using techniques that show us how to act in ways that do not let them stop or drive us	Go beyond fear because of our trust in the universe and our place in it
Reduce our stress levels using techniques that include retraining our neural pathways	Find the grace of equanimity in the midst of stress, a calm abiding in any circumstance, free of drama

How Far the Ego Can Go	*Where the Self Can Take Us*
Act justly toward others but come down hard on those who hurt us	Act generously toward others, even those who have hurt us
Demand restitution when we are taken advantage of; retribution is legitimate	Ask for amends but let go without ill will if it is not forthcoming; forgiveness is appropriate
Forgive when the other is repentant	Forgive whether or not the other is repentant, while not excusing the wrong done to us
All of this is limited; it is what is expected. It is achievable by work on ourselves.	*All of this transcends limits; it is more than what is expected. It happens because of grace to, through, and in ourselves.*

11

Graces in Relationships

Escaping resentment and becoming generous, escaping
arrogance and becoming humble, escaping self-concern
and becoming concerned about others: Personal transformations of this kind are not the work of flesh and blood,
they are the gifts of grace.

—GREGORY BAUM, FROM AN INTERVIEW,
"FAITH, COMMUNITY AND LIBERATION,"
IN THE *Journal of Philosophy and Scripture*

As human beings who take action, we live at two levels: essentially,
as we are in our being, and existentially, as we act in our here-
and-now doings. Both are necessary; one is not superior to the other.
Our *essential* reality, our being as members of the human species, is
unconditional, not affected by anything that can happen to us. We
are all humans no matter what we do or feel. However, it is also true that
we differ in how we express our humanity. That expression is condi-
tional upon how aware, just, and loving we are in the way we think
and act. That is the *existential* reality, how our being shows up in any
given moment. The Dalai Lama reported that he can suddenly become
quite angry. He then added: "So I am not yet fully human." Thus, our

essential humanity is always complete; our existential humanity takes work to complete.

We can apply the essential/existential distinction to our relationships. At the level of being, we have an irrepressible and uninterruptible capacity for love, for continuous caring connection, with no conditions or cautions. This unconditional being-centered potential for love is a gift capacity in all of us. It has nothing to do with our childhood or our life experiences. It cannot be erased by time, by anything that happened to us, or by anyone in our story. This capacity is grace.

The love in our true nature is not an ability like swimming or whittling. Those are talents we possess, but they are not essential to our being. Love, on the other hand, is a capacity and quality of our very being.

According to Saint Thomas Aquinas, in his *Summa Theologica,* our ineradicable inner goodness is based on grace: "The goodness in human nature is in its suitability and aptitude for grace and that goodness can never be lost, not even by sin." It follows that loving or praying for our enemies shows that we still believe in the power of grace to effect reconciliation. Then our practice becomes never giving up on anyone. Love pushes for exhibition. We *are* love, at the essential level, and that love can't be satisfied until it makes an appearance in daily life at an existential level. Each day we live, each circumstance that happens, each person we encounter, offers us an opportunity to activate our capacity and show our love in the here and now. Perhaps love is why we are alive today, why things happen, and why we meet the people we meet.

All of this is reminiscent of the Buddhist teaching that we are already enlightened and always have inherent goodness. Our bodhisattva practice is to manifest our enlightenment in our life here and now so we can share it with everyone. This is not as difficult as it sounds, since goodness wants to diffuse itself. All we have to do is move in rhythm with that natural movement already in us. The practice is simply allowing, simply aligning.

We can see an example of how this works in the virtue of generosity. We have a capacity for generosity, and we can manifest it in acts of giving. We remain essentially generous, even when we are not giving, because generosity is an ineradicable energy, a quality inside us. Like love, however, it keeps pushing to be released into conscious choices, to be shown in existential moments. Something in us wants us to demonstrate our ongoing generosity in every passing day and every situation.

Our capacity for love has nothing to do with how other people treat us or whether we like them. This is why the statement "Love your enemies" makes spiritual sense.

Our essential, being-level love is unconditional and universal in its extent. It does not have to be directed to specific people only. Love is what we are, so it can't be limited or preferential. When we believe we can love only certain people, we are not trusting our full capacity for love. We are mistakenly making existential, here-and-now choices that restrict the expression of the limitless—essential—potential that is in us.

With practice we can open the heart's door. The only tragedy is arriving at the evensong of life without having shown to everyone all the love we have. We still have all the time we need to run the risk of unconditionally loving. We all have the grace to do so.

We are also the objects of others' love. When others love us—a grace indeed—we feel an opening in ourselves. We might not have known our value until others loved us. Love is then doing what grace does: We did not have to work for it. We only had to be ourselves and it came through to us. We then easily love in return and become conduits of grace to others.

As friends share burdens with one another, they become stronger and wiser thanks to one another's support. When we look carefully at our friends, however, we definitely notice that they also have deficits and limitations. So the gift that comes to us from them must actually have come *through* them.

Love is not comfortable for very long in an atmosphere of perfection. It focuses on surfaces that are dented or scarred. Through those imperfections we enter the profound earthy depths where love takes root. In fact, there would be no chance for love to happen if the perfect were possible. There would be no one who needed caring connection. Thus, there is something about friendship, community, caring connection, that releases and transmits grace. It is like the transmission of the dharma; it does not come from the teacher but through him or her—and often from the least likely of sources.

> Human salvation lies in the hands of the creatively malad-justed.
>
> —MARTIN LUTHER KING JR., *Strength to Love*

Intimate Companions

We have certainly noticed that our mental image of the perfect partner is not always matched by the person with whom we fall in love or with whom we are in a relationship now.

The intimate relationships in our lives are often about what we need to learn more than they are about what we think we need. Through relationships we come face-to-face with ourselves, our needs, our childhood issues, our fears, our concealed or unknown shadow side. These lessons are graces that come to us through relationships.

Our earliest needs from childhood were attention, acceptance, appreciation, affection, allowing. These are the same needs we bring to adult intimate relationships. Intimacy is, in fact, the giving and receiving of what I've called the five A's, ways love is shown within an ongoing committed bond.* Both giving and receiving are about gifting. Each of these five A's is a grace in the sense that each is a gift we give to others and can receive from them.

- *Attention* is the gift of an engaged focus on one another, our feelings, our concerns, our future.
- *Acceptance* is the gift of openness to who each of us really is and to the choices each of us makes without a reaction of judgment or censure by the other.

---

* My most recent book, *How to Be an Adult in Love: Letting Love in Safely and Showing It Recklessly* (Shambhala Publications, 2013) explores the five A's as they apply to others and to ourselves.

- *Appreciation* is the gift of acknowledging and valuing who each of us is and what we do.
- *Affection* is the gift of nurturant bodily responsiveness to one another.
- *Allowing* is the gift of respect for one another's freedom, with no attempt by either of us to control the other.

These affirmations help us understand how love and grace are related in our interchange of the five A's:

I am a conduit of grace when I give someone the five A's.

The other person is a conduit of grace to me when I receive the five A's from him or her.

The five A's are how we stay with ourselves and others and how others stay with us. Thus the A's add up to an assisting force, the grace that summarizes and contains all five A's: *accompaniment.*

To accompany is to stay present. We stay with ourselves in our empty times; we stay with others in their troubled times. This connection helps free us from the isolation that makes crises so terrifying. "I'll get by as long as I have you" is a way of saying that we can survive better on the dark side of the moon when someone joins us there, holds our hand, is with us, beside us, for us—just what grace is about.

Here are some ways we become channels of graces to one another when darkness falls:

- We stay with one another in crises with levelheadedness and without giving advice.
- We pay attention to what the other says he needs, rather than what we think he needs.
- We do what we do out of the goodness of our hearts, not because the other earned it.
- We ask no recompense or reciprocation; the other is not obliged to us.
- We give of ourselves to someone even when she does not say "Thank you" or appreciate our gift, and then we cheerfully do it again.

- We keep giving the five A's to someone who may not give them to us.
- We do something kind without letting the other person know that it was we who did it.
- We behave generously or lovingly beyond the call of duty.

All of this happens within ourselves too when we apply these practices to how we hold ourselves in our own difficult times. We are then channels of grace to ourselves.

Grace is a gift to which we can say yes or no. Love, however, is only yes, an act of will, a commitment to do all that it takes for a caring connection to continue. That yes is how we give to others what grace bestows on us.

Discovering the Metaphor

> The outer event becomes metaphor to the inner world of the psyche.
>
> —ALICE O. HOWELL, *Jungian Synchronicity in Astrological Signs and Ages*

One way to appreciate the depth of the grace dimension in a relationship is to see it as a metaphor. Most of us are fundamentalists, taking the meaning of a special person in our lives only literally. We focus our attention on someone based on what this person does and on our impressions of her or him.

An alternative style is to focus also on the hidden meaning of what a partner represents in our mind and what our relationship with her or him is really about. We then find out more about who we really are. The same is true from our partner to us; this person is finding out who she or he is by being with us. Thus, a metaphorical meaning is more than—transcends—the literal one. That *more* is the clue to the presence of grace.

Here is an example. We notice that our partner is caregiving toward us in a motherly way. We find this annoying and engulfing. We complain about it to her as if it were entirely her choice and fault. In the realm of metaphor, however, we have mutually created and are reacting to a parent-child archetype. In some way, each of us needed to confront that archetype in ourselves, perhaps to look at still-unresolved experiences from our childhood. The metaphor continues when we realize that the relationship is not simply about two people living together in one house (literal). A relationship is a crucible (metaphor) in which we can finish some of our unfinished emotional business from the distant past. We find that opportunity by exploring the metaphorical meaning of our partner and relationship. That is a gift because it points us to important work on ourselves. We might say we find an opening into closure. We open to the significance of someone in the present; we find a clue to what needs closure from the past.

A relationship is not only about two individuals but also about how each of them has located exactly the partner who will re-create the past. We find ourselves with someone who brings up old joys and hurts, who fulfills or fails our needs, who blesses or disappoints us just as one or both of our parents did. The grace dimension of relationship then becomes clear.

Partners come forward as real persons only when this part of the work is embraced. Then a new metaphor can emerge, not one tied to the past, but one in which we are fully present in the moment and have thus found the grace of liberation from the past.

Our love for one another is likewise a metaphor for what the whole world really needs. Our caring connection is a microcosm of what the world is supposed to look like. We find the grace of locating a spiritual future of our partnership: a passionate concern for the wider world. This is how an appreciation of metaphor can ferry us to a universal loving consciousness.

Nothing was ever about only me or only this; it was always about a bigger picture, a picture of more.

To find the graces in a relationship that is ongoing or one that has ended, we can play with letting the other person become symbolic as described above. He or she is a metaphor for what it takes or took for both of us to evolve, to move along on our journey through life.

To see others metaphorically is to align to what the healthy psyche is doing through everyone we meet. Our deeper self casts people into teaching positions. Each person we meet and relate to shows us something about human nature and the depth of our own needs and inclinations. This applies to historical characters too. Hitler and Mother Teresa are not images in our psyches of a German leader and a nun in India. They have become symbols of the extremes of dark and light possibilities in us. As we saw above, there is both light and dark in all beings. The light and dark are not polarities; they are correlatives, so we need both to be whole.

We can easily accept how our psyche does this casting and symbolizing process in dreams, but we do not usually recognize its happening in other areas. In reality, every person is both himself or herself and a symbol meant to spur us to evolve in some way. This is one way the grace opportunity of relationship comes through to us. To concentrate on someone just as the person he presents himself to be deducts from the larger value he has in our story.

Finally, in a mature loving bond we see beyond the physical to the deeper beauty of the one we love. We see a value not noticed by those who do not love our partner as we do. This is not because love is blind but because we are in the gifted and gifting world where hyperboles are truths and metaphors are real.

When Conflicts Arise

How do grace and effort work together in the daily conflicts and issues that arise in a love relationship? It is a grace to meet a partner. It takes effort to keep the relationship going: We have to be willing to deal with the conflicts that arise between us. We are called upon to keep agreements with one another. We have to beware of our inclination to retaliate against one another; instead, we keep opening dialogues. We have to show feelings without aggression and receive those of our partner with appreciation. Graces will keep coming through in each of these challenges. The graces will help us begin, persevere, and complete our commitment to show our love.

Grace is the gift that comes to us without conditions, that is, with no need for a stack of merits, with no memory of prior offenses. This is how love works also. It does not have to be earned or won; it is a gift we give one another freely. Thus grace is what makes love unconditional, and effort is what makes a commitment enduring.

Conflicts arise in any relationship, whether with friends or at work or in intimate relationships. When conflicts arise, our psychological work is to address the issue together, processing the feelings and familiar past issues it evokes. This leads to making new agreements so that similar conflicts do not arise later.

We sometimes, however, react defensively and become fixated in how right we are and how wrong the other person is. We take the words or actions of the other person as the throwing down of a gauntlet, a challenge to a duel. We become oppositional, blaming, adversarial—the style of the untamed ego.

As we look for the grace dimension in relationships, we turn from ego to our deeper self, our true nature. There we find love, wisdom, and healing, the grace dimensions of our being. These can be applied to our conflicts. Our challenge is to look for the opportunity in a conflict to show love, to find wise solutions, and to bring about healing reconciliation. This is how we open to the graces that can emerge from our problems with others. We find the grace-moved self in us that stands behind our unmoving ego.

This style of bringing our true nature to a conflict makes opposition look complementary. Here is an example: We hear a person at work offer a way of doing something that is different from our way. Instead of defending our choice, we open to how her idea *adds* to ours rather than contradicts it. We are then more likely to look for ways to combine our ideas so we can do something cooperatively that is more effective than what either of us might have done on our own. Now the original suggestion from the other person has become an opportunity for creating a complete result rather than a one-sided one. What is coming at us from the other person helps us see another side of ourselves, a new possibility in attitude—it thus shows us ways of complementing our sense of ourselves.

This concept is familiar to us from our work with our shadow. We withdraw our projections onto others, and that helps us find parts of ourselves that were hidden from our conscious mind. We also take the projections of others onto us as information about where our own repressed side, our shadow side, lies hidden. Both of these forms of working with projections, from ourselves onto others or from others onto us, give us opportunities to find out more about who we are. In that sense working with projections opens us to grace, that is, to finding the riches in our life with others.

The Graces of Mature Love in a Relationship

We saw above that there are graces in our meeting our past in present relationships and in what we gain from working through conflicts. What are the directly positive features of an intimate relationship that can be considered graces? These are the beneficial qualities and fortuitous experiences that happen naturally as the relationship matures. Thus they are not based on effort but arise from the bond itself. They are the *felt* indicators of transcendent presence, the *more* that is afoot beyond what ego could ever have devised:

- We feel an ongoing gratitude for our presence in each other's lives.
- We go beyond our usual limits of generosity.
- We operate from selflessness rather than being motivated by reciprocity or reward.
- We care about each other as if our own interests were equal to those of our partner.
- We are always there for each other, willing to go the extra mile.
- We are open to each other's feelings no matter how messy.
- Everything we do or that happens can be held in the container of attention, acceptance, appreciation, affection, allowing.
- We always want the best for the other.
- We consider each other as under one another's care.
- We forgive every time.

- We find humor in our predicaments and personality quirks.
- Our inclination toward revenge has disappeared.
- We feel each other's presence even when we are apart.
- We feel safe and secure in the relationship no matter what the external events.
- Our embodied presence includes the erotic and goes beyond it at the same time.
- We continually sacrifice our own ego for the greater good of the relationship.
- No one can break in to wreck our bond.
- We feel as if our personal journey includes our partner as a necessary and welcome companion.
- We feel ever more openness, in and between ourselves, with every passing day and chapter of our life together.
- Our spiritual perspectives and practices are aligned.
- We let go when the time is right.

Things are losing their hardness; even my body now lets the light through.

—VIRGINIA WOOLF, *The Waves*

12

Spiritual Practices That Help
Us Open to Grace

Since all things are naked, clear from obscurations, there is
nothing to attain or realize. The everyday practice is simply to develop a complete acceptance and openness to all
situations and emotions and to all people, experiencing everything totally without reservations or blockages, so that
one never withdraws or centralizes into oneself.

— CHÖGYAM TRUNGPA RINPOCHE AND
RIGDZIN SHIKPO, "The Way of Maha Ati"

Practicing diving leads to an increase in skill. Practicing assertive-
ness results in greater self-esteem. In the realm of physical or psychological skills, we are guaranteed some success if we keep practicing.
Spiritual practices, however, do not guarantee an influx of grace. Grace
is a free spirit that visits both those who practice and those who do not.
The practices in the list below are therefore not ways of attaining grace.
They are ways of placing ourselves in an optimal position for grace to
unfold in us and come through to us. Our work is to open ourselves to
everything and not to manufacture anything. We are actually all being

helped by grace all the time, but we may not notice it. The more attention we pay to the moment, the more we will see grace at work. All we
have to know is how to open to the unique greeting, happy or sad, in
each moment. This is why spiritual practices always emphasize the importance of the here and now, the two glowing thresholds into the
world of grace. Our work is nothing other than opening to that world.

This openness is a wholehearted disposition of receptivity. Since
our life is a continual evolving, we are real only when we are open. *I
open, therefore I am.*

Here are some qualities of openness:

- Playfulness: good-natured mirth, hospitality toward surprises,
  irreverence toward absolutes, optimism, spontaneity, not taking
  things or ourselves too seriously
- Attunement to what is emerging in ourselves, in our
  relationships, in the world around us
- Presence in the here and now with utter fidelity to its raw
  realness, all wishful thinking dismissed
- Aligning ourselves to reality just as it depicts itself, no matter
  how surprising or discomfiting
- Confidence in our own ineradicable goodness and creativity
  so that we keep trusting what is within us beyond our
  conditioning, projections, biases
- Inclusiveness toward both people and ideas
- Letting go of what we hold on to for safety and security; we
  recall Meister Eckhart: "Everything is meant to be let go of
  that the soul may stand in unhampered nothingness."
- Revealing, to someone we trust, the facts and feelings about
  ourselves that we have kept secret because they do not match
  the persona we want to exhibit
- Greeting events in our lives with the five A's:

    1. We are attentive to the graces that lead to and support
       our calling.

2. We accept—accommodate, receive—whatever happens, whether it arrives in positive or negative forms. This helps us recognize and find whatever gift may be in it.
3. We appreciate the manifold ways that powers beyond ourselves are always and everywhere offering graces to us.
4. We show these powers affectionately.
5. We allow them their full and far-reaching impact on our lives and relationships.

- We ask for graces in prayer and affirmation. Thus, we practice what we seek. For instance, we place an intention for *bodhicitta,* a grace, but we renew our bodhisattva vows daily, our practice.
- We engage in some intentional silence each day. This does not mean simply not talking. It is stillness with an attitude of listening, yet with no expectation of hearing anything. Our mental chatter is also a form of distracting noise. We cannot stop the endless train of thoughts in our heads. Silence in this area will mean simply letting our thoughts flow through without attaching to them or forcibly expelling them. We remain focused on our breathing as thoughts come and go. We do not turn to watch their path but let them pass by as we remain still.

From silence comes *beholding*—not simply seeing, but seeing into. Our listening gaze is free of all former influences or programming. We are present purely, only here, only now, with only this. In such silent stillness we open the part of our brain that allows intuitions to come through. We respond by paying close attention. How do we know the voice we hear is that of grace?

- It will be freeing, not controlling, contracting, or coercive.
- It will sound like a new voice, not our own ego voice.
- It will come not from left-brain logic but from a sudden or growing intuitive realization.
- It cannot be argued against.
- It is unforgettable and yet indescribable.

- It will feel right all over: body, mind, heart, gut.
- It will match up with messages that have been coming through to us in dreams and synchronicities.
- We will experience clear discernment, an automatic ability to see into what happens. We see this realization in words from "The Dark Night of the Soul" by the Spanish mystic poet Saint John of the Cross: "I journeyed but without the help of my mind; yet there was a light within that led me."

We can also empower our intention for opening ourselves with statements like these:

- I see that fear comes up in me when I become attached to the illusion that everything depends on what I do.
- I so easily lose touch with the wonderful resources of grace that want to come through to me.
- I am beginning to notice and welcome the many graces that have come and are coming to me, especially from connections with those who love me. This moves me from controlling to allowing.
- I do not become attached to moving myself; I let movement and stillness happen in their own time.

May I always be open to the graces that surround me.
May I be thankful for the graces that everywhere enwind me.
May love flow through me and become a grace to everyone around me.

Showing Gratitude

The gifts or blessings of life are always there but if we are not aware of them, they don't do much for us. That is where gratefulness comes in. Gratefulness makes us aware of the gift and makes us happy.

—BROTHER DAVID STEINDL-RAST, FROM AN INTERVIEW WITH HENRY STARK IN *Sacred Journey*

Grace and gratitude have something in common. Grace is something given, not something that is due us. Gratitude is a response to what is given as a gift, not to what we have earned or what is due to us.

Some of us can recall a dictum from our public school education: "Don't expect a reward for doing your duty." The concept here is that we cannot expect thanks for fulfilling obligations. Indeed, gratitude is only for something undue, that is, over and above what is expected or owed. For instance, when a cashier gives us change for a purchase, we might say "Thank you" to be polite, but we do not *feel* gratitude, since we are receiving what is owed to us. If the cashier gives us a coupon toward future purchases, then we might feel and express authentic gratitude.

At the same time, in other interchanges, we feel grateful when people fulfill obligations to us. This is because it is a given of life that not everyone is dutiful, so we feel grateful to those who do indeed respect us by being so. People sometimes do not receive what we do for them with gratitude. Instead, they may seem more entitled than appreciative. This same unfortunate reaction can happen with respect to grace. The experience of receiving graces becomes negative when we take graces as entitlements rather than as gifts.

Appreciation is acknowledgement and gratitude. Thus, to appreciate grace and truly open to it requires an awareness of and gratitude for ongoing graces and expressions of thanks for occasional graces. Then we do not interpret graces as signs that we have a charmed life and that we can thus do anything we want without consequences. That comes across as entitlement rather than appreciation. "I open to grace by my gratitude for all the ways it is already happening."

Gratitude can be a lifestyle, an atmosphere in the ecology of our lives. This idea is expressed well by the Tibetan Buddhist teacher Chögyam Trungpa. He refers to compassion as an "environmental generosity," that is, not having a separate subject or object. In enlightened consciousness, there is no one having compassion or receiving it, only compassion happening in response to suffering going on in the here and now. Likewise with gratitude, there is no subject or object of gratitude, only the attitude of thanks pervading our consciousness in each moment.

The practice of such gratitude in attitude might sound like this: "I feel a sense of gratefulness. It does not seem entirely of my own making. It has a graced quality. I feel a permeation of gratefulness, all through me. This heartfelt gratitude feels inspiring and nourishes me. In some mysterious way, grace has become the same as gratitude."

We can summarize much of what we have learned about grace so far by using the acrostic EASES. This can be a useful trigger for remembering the scope of our gratitude. Grace *eases* our journey. Grace

- *E*mpowers us
- *A*ctivates us
- *S*upplements us
- *E*nlightens us
- *S*upports us

What is your way of showing thanks?

- How are you thankful for each of the five qualities of grace: empowering, activating, supplementing, enlightening, supporting?
- How can your gratitude endure in these five ways during or after negative events?
- How can you be a conduit of grace to others in these same five ways? True gratitude is followed by generosity; we give back as our response to having been given to.

As I write, the Olympics have just ended in London. I am musing on how the original athletes in ancient Greece were sure to thank the gods for their laurel crowns. For instance, in the *Olympiad X* of *The Odes of Pindar,* we read: "A man, with the assistance of God's hand, can push to great glory." I am wondering how many of the medalists now have that sense of gratitude for their success toward an assisting power beyond their own grit. We usually think of athletic skill as based entirely on years of practice and on imagining oneself winning. We rarely include a recognition of graces as components of victory. Yet the graces certainly began when the athlete was born with a capacity for a sport, found his or her interest in that sport, and received the support and encouragement of parents and coaches to play that sport.

As an aside, we notice that our talents may not activate without encouragement, without the five A's, from those around us. This is an indicator of the importance of connection in our creativity and personal development.

For those who were encouraged, the graces kept working in manifold unknown ways on the road that led to the Olympics. What are we losing out on when we don't acknowledge those grace-filled elements in the gold?

Later, by the way—or shall I say, by a graceful synchronicity—I happened to hear an interview with Nancy Hogshead-Makar, a gold medalist for swimming in the 1984 Olympics. She said: "You feel that graced quality when you are really good at something. . . . It feels effortless." She seemed to me to be acknowledging grace in her victory.

I thought how all of us can feel gratitude for the graced quality of all we have going for us. Nancy's statement also reminded me of how often we notice grace unfolding *because* what we do feels effortless. Grace is mobile, so effortlessness, with its sense of free flow, is certainly a sign of grace in action. In addition, when we act from grace we are indeed artless in another sense: We have no motive but to align ourselves with what wants to happen. We trust the path opened by grace, and we trust opening to it.

As we realize that psychology and spirituality work together in every area of life, we acknowledge the role of grace in our choice to live a responsible life. Such a commitment does not maintain itself by our effort and willpower alone. We are being assisted in our psychological work in the same three areas as in spiritual practice: at the moment of choosing, throughout the experiencing, and in the fulfillment. We are also assisted in our talent and sports careers in the same three ways. To show awareness of this makes gratitude a spiritual practice. Perhaps a time will come when our practice of showing thanks will lead to our feeling that we have become gratitude. Indeed, every spiritual practice is meant to move us from performing actions to awakening to who we really are.

> Grace and gratitude go together like heaven and earth.
>
> —KARL BARTH, *Church Dogmatics*

Accepting the Givens of Life

> The quirks of life,
> With all the pain they bring us,
> Teach us not to hang on
> To this floating world.
>
> —IKKYU SOJUN (1394–1481)

Gautama Buddha grew up living a sheltered life, unaware of the incontrovertible givens of life in the world around him. When he finally entered the workaday world, he was confronted with three surprising and perplexing realities: sickness, old age, and death. Each of these alerted him to facts he needed to contemplate and accept. Since this experience led him ultimately to enlightenment, we can say that the three facts were three challenges with opportunities, conduits of grace. Each was a messenger with significant information about the spiritual path.

In addition to these three surprising facts, Gautama experienced a clash of contrasts: He saw a sick person, and he himself was healthy. He saw an old person, and he himself was young. He saw a dead person, and he himself was alive. This combination of opposites helped him cross the threshold into spiritual consciousness. When we notice how apparent opposites coincide, we have entered the world of meaningful coincidence, synchronicity. This is the realm of grace.

The Buddha's confrontation with more than what he knew previously was not something otherworldly but rather the bare-bones reality of all existing beings. Many graced realizations, however, flowed from his awakening to that reality. He realized that unreliability, unsatisfactoriness, and impermanence are unalterable givens of life.

Our wisest response then is to let go of attachment to anything, since it would be unrealistic and would lead to the suffering of disappointment and frustration. We still want things, and we continue to relate to people. We don't renounce or dismiss what seems appealing. We simply give up the grabbing and clinging. We do what the transcendent does: We go beyond without abandoning. We go beyond while including. We do not reject what we love. We hold what we love without squeezing.

The Buddha recommended the sacrifice of attachment as a path to enlightenment. The brilliant spiritual irony is that letting go of attachment leads to an acceptance of unreliability, unsatisfactoriness, and impermanence as facts of life. When we cease quarreling with those givens, we find the gift of equanimity. Thus we become content with reality as it is. We notice that we have found the grace to live with the truth of suffering without a quarrel. This was stated in such a robust and folksy way by Aunt Eller in the 1955 film *Oklahoma:* "You got to get used to having all kinds of things happening to you. You got to look at all the good on the one side and all the bad on the other side and say: 'Well, all right then to both of you!'"

The givens of life are incontestable facts, laws of existence, how things work on this planet and in our lives, whether or not we agree and no matter how we protest. They are unavoidable, unpredictable, beyond our control, defying our plans and wishes. They require a fully adult response rather than a sugar-coated one. That response can only be an unconditional yes.

In my book *The Five Things We Cannot Change,* I list some central givens:

1. Things change and end.
2. Life does not always proceed in accord with our plans.
3. Suffering is part of everyone's life.
4. Life is not always fair.
5. People are not loving and loyal all the time.

Each of these is indeed a given—and *given,* that is, a gift given to us, since each contains an opening for growth. Each one can stretch us into the lofty dimensions of our humanity: character, depth, and compassion. The practice of yes to each given becomes an access to grace, since thereby we let go of a specific illusion:

- The fact that things change and end helps us find the grace to let go of the illusion of permanence. We then grieve for what is lost or gone, so we can say good-bye, which turns out to be the open sesame to moving on with our lives.
- When plans fall apart, we find the grace to let go of the illusion of control and open ourselves to what may next arise to challenge and develop us.
- Suffering helps us grow in compassion for ourselves and for those who suffer as we do. We find the grace to let go of the illusion of exemption, of the belief that what happens to anyone else cannot happen to us. We find the gift of compassion for those who suffer more or less than we.
- As we accept the fact of unfairness in life, we find the grace to let go of the illusion that we are guaranteed fair treatment all the time. We see how injustice hurts, and we don't perpetrate it on others. We feel healthy grief as an alternative to our primitive reaction to injustice of seeking revenge. We no longer feel like victims but rather like everyone else in the human family, all of us facing the same givens.
- Our realization that people are not always loving and loyal to us shows us we cannot trust everyone. We find the grace to let go of the illusion that everyone is supposed to be true to us. We learn that betrayal can help us let go of the illusion that an intimate relationship will necessarily be trustworthy. As we grow in spiritual consciousness, what comes to matter most is not to hurt others but to act with integrity and trustworthiness toward them no matter how they act toward us.

These realizations and commitments are signs of spiritual progress. When we acknowledge each given as a grace, our locus of safety and security shifts from others to ourselves. We accept the fact, without bitterness, that we cannot always trust life to give us what we want or expect people to be what we want them to be. We learn to place our trust in reality just as it is, an uneven tapestry of satisfactions and disappointments. That is the equivalent of grounding ourselves, what makes it possible to trust ourselves.

Grounding here can be interpreted in two senses: We are stabilized on firm ground, no longer shaken by ego fears and cravings. We have ground down our stories and concepts so that only what is down-to-earth real remains.

Each given of life arouses feelings. Our feelings are our innate bodily technologies for handling the hurts, betrayals, and disappointments we meet up with in daily life. Each feeling capacity is a conduit of grace in that it helps us face what happens in each given so we can grieve and get on with life.

The three main feelings aroused by the givens of life are the components of grief:

1. We are sad about how unreliable life is, about what we missed out on or lost.
2. We are angry at the way life is or at those involved in what upsets us.
3. We are afraid things will not turn around or we will not be able to handle future predicaments. We are all so afraid of entering the unknown, yet it can hold so many graces.

Allowing ourselves to experience these feelings fully is how we engage and relate to our grief. We are saying yes unconditionally to each given and feeling. Notice that allowing ourselves to feel is a component of loving ourselves, one of the five A's that make us stronger. This is another way that our griefs are conduits to grace.

Our work with grief or any of our emotions proceeds skillfully when we follow these six steps:

1. We become aware of the sensations our feelings arouse in our bodies.

2. We name and distinguish our sensations and our feelings.

3. We see how they are familiar, evoked by past experiences going all the way back to early life.

4. We let ourselves fully feel our emotions, with no attempt to soften or escape their raw impact.

5. We experience our feelings without trying to fix, end, adjust, or flee them. This is usually unfamiliar, so we realize, perhaps for the first time, how much of what we thought was feeling was really mental elaboration, stories embroidered around our feelings. Our experience of our feelings helps us distinguish our story from the reality, a grace indeed.

6. We notice when we are judging our feelings as bad or wrong, interpreting them so they can fit our self-image or what people think of us. We let go of those interferences so we can be with our feelings just as they are. All it takes is welcoming and staying with whatever feeling comes up in any here and now. They all eventually go to ground, and we remain standing and grounded too.

With the liberation of our feelings from their mental baggage, we can relax. We then notice that our body widens to become a field of universal human experience. We suddenly realize that our emotions are identical to those of others all over the world who feel as we do. We have moved, or rather have been moved, to bring the personal to the universal so we transcend all divisions. Our feelings have led to a sense of connection with the wider world, and we feel compassion for those who suffer as we do. This is our shift of grace into the spiritual.

We can benefit from stating the following combined affirmation of and aspiration for loving-kindness as the day begins, as we begin work or recreation, as we go on a date, or at the beginning of any event in our day:

I say yes to everything that happens to me today as an opportunity to give and receive love without reserve.

I am thankful for the enduring capacity to love that has come to me from the Sacred Heart of the universe.

May everything that happens to me today open my heart more and more.

May all that I think, say, feel, and do express loving-kindness toward myself, those close to me, and all beings.

May love be my life purpose, my bliss, my destiny, the richest grace I can receive or give.

And may I always be especially compassionate toward people who are considered least or last or who feel alone or lost.

Cultivating Serenity, Courage, and Wisdom

There are three graces that stand out in the course of every human life: serenity, courage, and wisdom. Here is the original version of the prayer composed by Reinhold Niebuhr in 1943 that is now so popular in 12-step programs:

> God give us the grace to accept with serenity the things that cannot be changed, the courage to change the things that should be changed, and the wisdom to know the difference.

The prayer asks for three graces that reside in us as enduring capacities. Our practice then is to ask for an awakening of these graces that we already have in our enlightened nature. *Ask* in this context means placing an intention to release what is within us. The word *God* can refer to our true nature, the higher power always ready to arise in and through us. In this perspective, God is transcendent by being immanent in each of us. Joseph Campbell, in *The Hero with a Thousand Faces*, wrote: "The two worlds, the divine and the human . . . are actually one. The realm of the gods is a forgotten dimension of the world we know."

Our aspirations might be:

- May I open to the grace of serenity to accept what can't be changed.
- May I open to the grace of courage to change what I can change.
- May I open to the grace of wisdom to know the difference.

Since a practice is not about acquiring graces but about opening to them, our part is to identify and clear away the following obstructions to their full realization:

- We prevent ourselves from access to the grace of serenity when we are caught up in drama, live for an adrenaline rush, and endure stress and exhaustion at work or in a relationship with no letup.
- We lose contact with the grace of courage when we play it safe, never put ourselves on the line for what we believe in, hide our true feelings and outlook, do not take a stand for or give support to those who deserve it from us.
- We foreclose on access to the grace of wisdom when we live in illusion rather than align ourselves to reality. Our challenge as humans is to keep adjusting our relationship to reality until our thoughts, beliefs, and choices match it.

We all have the capacity to align ourselves with reality, to accept what cannot be changed. We say yes to what is rather than resisting how it is or quibbling with the way it is. Our attention is not fixed and obsessed but becomes softer in its gaze so we can see around reality and through it. Then a sense of letting go comes as a felt shift. That will feel like a grace, a result not caused by us, an opening into a newfound spaciousness. As we let go of resistance, space, time, and energy open automatically because it was only our own resistance that had been confining them anyway.

Letting Go of Self-Centeredness

The ego we let go of is not the healthy executive part of us that makes wise decisions and works toward reasonable goals. It is the neurotic, anxiety-driven, compulsive, ultimately fear-based tendency in us to focus only on our own needs and desires. This narcissistic ego operates on the basis of self-interest, control, and entitlement.

When we become ego invested in these unhealthy ways, we do harm to our spirituality because we cancel the possibility of feeling compassion. We are so caught up in ourselves that we miss many chances at love—and happiness.

We sometimes fear letting go of ego, as it may mean there will be nothing left of us. I recently removed a chair that had been in front of a window for a long time. For the first week, when I looked at the window area, it seemed as if something was *missing*. But later, now, it looks like *more space*. This is what happens with letting go of ego. At first it seems that something is missing. But in reality we have been given more space to be who we really are in our enlightened nature. And by the way, I did not *make* the change happen in my mind between believing something was missing and then finding more space. It just happened suddenly on its own—a metaphor for how grace works.

Here are some specific practices for reversing a self-centered ego style, all pathways to openness to grace:

- We affirm that other people matter and we take their needs into account in all of our decisions.
- We let ourselves show our vulnerability in intimate relationships.
- We let go of taking the reactions of others toward us too personally, which helps us understand them in kinder ways.
- We concentrate on giving the five A's more than on receiving them.
- When someone hurts us, we do not retaliate, but we do say "Ouch!" and sincerely attempt to open a dialogue. Reconciliation instead of retaliation evokes our compassion toward the other and perhaps the other's compassion toward us.
- We look for how any event or circumstance can be an opportunity to show loving-kindness and integrity.
- We release ourselves from our habit of control by respecting others' freedom.

- We commit ourselves to living in the here and now free of pre-conceived ideas or plans to force things to come out as we want them to. We let the chips fall where they may. We then make the best of the way they fell. We ask for, or place an intention for, the grace of transformation, realizing that we cannot let go of our anxiety-driven ego on our own.

A major hurdle in letting go of self-focus is controlling behavior. Our practice takes effort. When effort becomes control, it turns into compulsion, the poor person's version of control. Compulsion means we can't stop ourselves from behaving in ways that seem necessary but are actually meant to stave off anxiety. We also can't stop trying to make everything—and everyone around us—perfect. Compulsion is the shadow side of responsible action, the version that is so extreme that it causes stress and harm. Compulsion is driven by anxiety, not composure. The process may look like this:

1. Anxiety leads to panic or a need to end itself as soon as possible.
2. Anxiety includes feeling out of control.
3. So we imagine getting in control will fix the anxiety.

Actually, we can transform anxious compulsion into intelligent, well-paced work to reach a reasonable goal, in the following ways:

1. We pause and feel our anxiety fully.
2. We do not jump to controlling as the solution.
3. Instead, we make choices not driven or determined by the anxiety. We are not taking refuge in compulsion. In this way the anxiety lessens in its impact.
4. We end with an affirmation: "I let go of control and discover my real freedom." Our ego has always wanted this freedom from fear.

Now our self-worth is disconnected from whether we feel a sense of accomplishment or maintain serenity. Once we experience this inherent self-worth, we notice, also experientially, the workings of grace that animate and accompany our work. This is a release from the error that fuels compulsion: "I have nothing going for me but me." This is how an awareness of grace is a giant step toward freedom from the commands of a fear-based ego.

It is important to keep in mind that we let go of the self-centered ego not as a strategy to gain results but as way to open to grace. Thomas Merton, in a letter to the peace worker Jim Forest in 1966, wrote: "Do not depend on the hope of results. When you are doing the sort of work you have taken on . . . you may have to face the fact that your work will be apparently worthless and even achieve no result at all, if not perhaps results opposite of what you expect. As you get used to this idea, you start more and more to concentrate not on the results but on the value, the rightness, the truth of the work itself. . . . Then you can be more open to the power that will work through you without your knowing it."

The "power that will work through you" is grace.

Following the Eightfold Path

In Buddhism there are the Four Noble Truths that describe the path toward enlightenment:

1. There is suffering—unsatisfactoriness—in life, the first given of our existence.
2. The cause of suffering is attachment—the first strategy we choose to free ourselves from unsatisfactoriness.
3. There is a way to end suffering—our first opportunity, our first graced chance for healing and release.
4. The way is the Eightfold Path to enlightenment—our lifelong challenging practice.

The Eightfold Path describes what our true nature, buddha nature, looks like when it is fully operative in our lives.

The Eightfold Path offers practices that help free us from the attachment and craving that cause suffering. They are time-honored ways to develop an unconditional relationship to reality so that our delusions can end. Walpola Rahula, in *What the Buddha Taught*, called this reality orientation "seeing a thing in its true nature, without name or label."

The true nature of things—and of us—is impermanence and contingency rather than permanence and freestanding independent existence. We let go of attachment because there is nothing to attach to. We can safely relate to the world and to others, since everything is interconnected. It is unsafe, a cause of suffering, to cling to anything, since nothing is fixed or stable.

The practices of the Eightfold Path enumerated below are all interconnected, so we engage in them simultaneously, not sequentially. With a consciousness of synchronicity, we will notice that when we focus on one, the others automatically present themselves to us as daily challenges. When Snow White kissed one dwarf, the other six lined up right away.

The practices are meant to bring wholesomeness, wisdom, and skill to eight areas in our lives: our perspective (view), intention, speech, action, livelihood, effort, mindfulness, and concentration. The first two help us find wise insight. The next three challenge us to embrace ethical behavior. The final three offer mind-heart training toward enlightenment.

The ideal form of practice of each of the eight is traditionally referred to as "right," what we might now understand as wholesome, skillful, or wise. Each serves to open us to the action of grace in our lives because each reduces our ego's hold over us.

Right View

Right view is a perspective that sees the whole picture, that has a healthy outlook on life, an accurate understanding of how the world works, an optimism about humans that makes us never give up on them. Our optimism is about ourselves too. Both we and all others have the capacity for enlightenment and therefore for happiness. In this regard, we recall Saint Thomas Aquinas's similar recommendation that we never give up on believing in the transformation of anyone, because grace can come at any moment, even at the last one.

Right view also includes the realization that we are not separate from one another. We understand that our identity is only a designation. With a clear perspective, we come to see that all of us and all beings are one. This is what makes compassion not a sense of pity for those less fortunate than we but a sense of others as equal to us. The expression "There but for the grace of God go I" misses our sense of solidarity with humanity. A more accurate statement might be: "There, *by* grace, go I." Thus, compassion is not from one to another but in oneness with another. In right view there is no truly other. In fact, in any dealing with people, we meet ourselves. There is no self and other, only self with other.

It follows that a major focus in building a wholesome view of nature, humanity, and the world is seeing our oneness with all beings. This is how we free ourselves from separateness and grow in compassion.

Finally, right view is also about noticing that there are consequences to our actions. Then we may more likely become willing to receive and deal with the effects of our choices. This sense of personal responsibility is a way of maintaining our own integrity and our sense of accountability to others as well.

Right Intention

Right intention refers to clear and reality-oriented thinking. Joined to right view, it is a path to wisdom. View is cognitive; intention is voluntary. Intention in this context is about willpower, not mind power. So wholesome intention requires renunciation of aggression, aversion, and craving. Thus, there are three basic ways of increasing right intention:

1. We intend and choose the path of nonviolence in all of our dealings. Our commitment to nonviolence in all of our dealings opens us to the grace of universal and unbiased loving-kindness.

2. We show goodwill toward our own inner darkness and that of others so it can be befriended and transformed. We may find the shadow side repulsive, but we do not run from it. This is an opening to grace, because befriending our shadow side helps us accept our true self and that of others with realism and compassion.

3. We tame our primitive drive to be caught in desires that lead to craving. We do not attempt to end our desiring, a chimerical task. Instead we seek to discover how our drive/desire is ultimately about our yearning for the transcendent. Then the power of grace focuses us on what really matters to our spiritual evolution.

Regarding this third practice, we are actually severing the long-standing link between appeal or lack of it and our response. We no longer equate *pleasant* with "I have to have that" or *unpleasant* with "I have to avoid that." This is how we release ourselves from becoming too attached or repulsed, the cause of so much of our suffering. The danger of our preference for the pleasant and our flight from the unpleasant is that it leads to compulsion. Thereby our willpower evaporates and we lose our freedom. We also lose the element of surprise, so crucial to an openness to grace.

Right Speech

Right speech means not engaging in lies, abusive language, insult, sarcasm, slander, gossip. We do not engage in negative humor, that is, what is meant to shame others or is prejudiced against those who are different from ourselves. We speak up when others do so and ask them to cease. We want to use our speech in ways that honor everyone and that assertively protect those who are the butt of biased humor.

We no longer engage in chatter or meaningless superficial conversation. We are personable, engaging, and interactive. We still use speech for entertainment. But in serious dialogue we now say only what is true, helpful, timely, and necessary.

We are authentic, not deceptive. This means more than simply not saying what may harm others. We use our communication skills altruistically: to speak up about interpersonal, political, or religious injustice. We share our insights and seek to promote justice, peace, and love in all that we say. This is using speech to spread the dharma.

In his book *The Heart of the Buddha's Teaching*, the Vietnamese Zen teacher Thich Nhat Hanh says: "Deep listening is the foundation of Right Speech. If we cannot listen mindfully, we cannot practice Right Speech. No matter what we say, it will not be mindful, because we'll be speaking only our own ideas and not in response to the other person."

A commitment to right speech is an opening to grace because we notice the dharma of loving-kindness coming through in our communications with everyone, even without our planning to have it happen that way.

Right Action

Right action refers to behavior that is morally upright. This means following precepts not to lie, kill, steal, abuse intoxicants, or behave irresponsibly, especially in our sexuality. These precepts outline the lifestyle of an enlightened person. As we live in harmony with the world and with others, we naturally act in caring and respectful ways as profiled in healthy moral precepts.

Our commitment to ethical and skillful action also includes cultivating social consciousness, a caring connection to society. By grace, this caring connection continually expands so it can include all the world, its ecology, and its peoples.

Thich Nhat Hanh says in *The Heart of the Buddha's Teaching*: "The basis of Right Action is to do everything in mindfulness." He proposes five mindfulness trainings based on and summarizing the precepts:

1. Respect for life: We do not hurt others, and we protect living things.

2. Generosity: We share our gifts, time, and resources in response to the needs of others. We do not exploit others for our own profit. We stand for and promote equality for all.

3. Sexual responsibility: We honor our own and others' relationships and keep our commitment to act with loving-kindness and responsibility. We do not exploit others for our own sexual gain.

4. Loving speech and deep listening: We do not engage in language that causes discord or hate. We listen attentively to others so we can feel our deep connection to them. We are not divisive in our speech.

5. Avoidance of intoxicants: We are careful about what we consume, preferring healthful foods over those that harm us. We do not misuse drugs that cause addiction. We are also cautious about what we let into our minds from TV or other forms of entertainment.

Right Livelihood

Right livelihood refers to engaging in work that is based on right action. It is work or a career that benefits others and the planet. We are committed to do no harm, to act ethically in business, not to cheat others or take advantage of them. This means not being engaged in work that deals in weaponry or intoxicants or that hurts people or nature in any way.

Thich Nhat Hanh also says in *Heart of the Buddha's Teaching,* "To practice Right Livelihood, you have to find a way to earn your living without transgressing your ideals of love and compassion. The way you support yourself can be an expression of your deepest self, or it can be a source of suffering for you and others. . . . Our vocation can nourish our understanding and compassion, or erode them. We should be awake to the consequences, far and near, of the way we earn our living."

The Vipassana teacher S. N. Goenka says in *The Buddha and His Teachings:* "If the intention is to play a useful role in society in order to support oneself and to help others, then the work one does is right livelihood." This commitment is to the kind of work, career, or volunteering that is oriented toward compassionate service.

In addition, in wise livelihood we relate fairly and cooperatively to our fellow workers. We are always asking this question about work and our dealings with others: "How can this serve my practice?" The practice is mindfulness, loving-kindness, and this Eightfold Path.

Right Effort

Right effort is about exercising due diligence in our practices. Even if we are weary, we persevere, exerting ourselves assiduously to keep our thoughts, words, and deeds conscientious. This means maintaining a discipline that keeps us on track without becoming masochistic. We check our distracting tendency to slack off, and that arouses our healthy inclination to stay on the path.

Effort in this context is curbing and training our ego to enter the service of our enlightened nature. The inner move to value what may enlighten us happens by the action of grace. It is beyond the ego's control but enlists the ego in its best work: to establish a synergistic relationship with the powers in our own true nature.

The right amount of effort means exerting just enough energy and neutrality to see reality as it is rather that be caught in either an obsession about it or a disregard of it. We find a balance rather than go to an extreme. This balance reminds us of the *more* at work than just our own exertions. This is how we open to grace *through* our efforts.

Commitment to practices, that is, the exerting of effort, shows that we have the capacity to work on change. This does not mean get in control and stay there but put energy into what calls for change and then let go. We then avoid the activism that thrives on controlling and the quietism that becomes paralyzed by passivity. Our goal is like the correct tuning of a guitar, not too constricted or too loose. Each of the practices in this chapter, and especially in this Eightfold Path, is a tweak of the guitar of ourselves as we engage in practice.

Right Mindfulness

Right mindfulness is alert awareness of the here and now. It's when we notice what is happening in the present moment without the embroideries stitched in by our ego. This is bare attention without clinging to or rejecting our thoughts, only noticing them, aware of their impermanence. Mindfulness helps us let go of clinging by increasing our loyalty to that awareness. *Do I mostly limit or welcome what the moment presents me?*

As we work with our faculty of cognition so that we see with clarity, we notice graces coming to us: We are not so easily enticed by our moods or projections. We have become fair and alert witnesses of all that happens—not judges and juries of what happens. This frees us from the illusion of separateness—just what it takes to feel authentic compassion.

Mindfulness as focused awareness of the here and now, combined with accurate comprehension of what is happening, is an antidote to ignorance and delusion. Mindfulness stabilizes us in reality, that is, it grants us presence of mind.

Even if we experience one distracting thought after another, our meditation is still valuable because we are still seeing exactly how our mind works. Thus, there is no way to engage in mindfulness meditation incorrectly as long as we just stay put. The sitting, not doing or going, means we are with ourselves in the moment, as we are and as it is, without running away from ourselves. To sit is to give up all hideouts. This is because sitting in meditation is the one time we can't get away from ourselves. Our commitment to that is all it takes for success at meditation.

The word *mindfulness* in English means attentive regard. The Pali word *sati*, translated as "mindfulness," literally means recollection. The word *sati* is from *sarati*, which means to remember. In fact, "recollection" and "retention" are more apt translations and descriptions of mindfulness in its original meaning.

Our modern view of mindfulness is as an attentiveness to the pure here and now, an awareness not embroidered by judgments or beliefs. We are simply aware of our thoughts and experience without attaching to them or rejecting them.

Returning to consciousness of our breathing is the method that reminds us to come back to the moment, since breath is only a here-and-now reality, with no past or future, unlike a thought-generated memory.

As a caveat, Muho Noelke, in a dharma talk given while he was abbot of the Japanese monastery Antaiji, declared: "We have to forget things like 'I should be mindful of this or that.' If you are mindful, you are already creating a separation: 'I-am-mindful-of—.' Don't be mindful, please! When you walk, just walk. Let the walk walk. Let the talk talk. Dogen Zenji says: 'When we open our mouths, it is filled with Dharma.' Let the eating eat, the sitting sit, the work work. Let sleep sleep."

Right Concentration

Right concentration is *samadhi,* a Sanskrit word meaning deep and absorbing contemplation. This is what we move toward in our commitment to ongoing meditation. In the Hindu yogic tradition, *samadhi* is considered the final phase of life, in which union with the divine manifests itself in us. It can happen before or after death.

In *samadhi* our mindfulness and clarity about the workings of our mind are so developed that we let go of self-critical or obsessive thoughts. We feel at ease about who we have been and are. This leads to equanimity, a form of fearlessness, since we are not intimidated by circumstances. We greet them as features of ourselves because they are part of our story. Hence, they are not alien and dangerous. We salute them with appreciation, since every predicament offers us an opportunity for awakening. The result is graces like these:

- We are serene in how we face and deal with what life may bring.
- We go through all that happens to us with even-mindedness.
- We are not overwhelmed by negative events or positive experiences but take them in stride.

- We are learning to recognize an awakening quality in all that happens to us.
- We feel compassion for those who suffer as we do.

In daily life right concentration refers to a level of single-mindedness that keeps us focused on wholesome thoughts, words, and deeds. No longer misunderstanding the nature of reality, we stay in contact with our own true nature, wise, enlightened, compassionate.

In the Maha-Cattarisaka Sutra we read about skillful concentration/ meditation: "The Blessed One said: 'Now what, monks, is noble right concentration with its supports and requisite conditions? Any single-ness of mind equipped with these seven factors—right view, right intention, right speech, right action, right livelihood, right effort, and right mindfulness—is called noble right concentration with its supports and requisite conditions.'" Thus, this practice contains all the others and supports them.

Epilogue

The Grace in Being Human

Grace is operative in the experience of infinite longings, of radical optimism, of unquenchable discontent, of our torment about the insufficiency of everything attainable, of the radical protest against death, the experience of being confronted with an absolute love precisely where it is lethally incomprehensible and seems to be silent and aloof, the experience of a radical guilt and of a still-abiding hope. These elements are in fact tributary to that divine force which impels the created spirit—by grace—to an absolute fulfillment. Hence in them grace is experienced as well as the natural being of a human life.

—ROGER HAIGHT, *The Experience and Language of Grace*

Grace is not an abstract concept or a twilight zone surreal experience. It is earthy, not otherworldly, in that it works through our senses, showing itself in concrete situations. Grace is transcendent, yet it contains me and you in every here and now. In this sense, the transcendent is within, not beyond, our human story.

Grace reveals how the spiritual is not the opposite of the material but aligns with it and works through it. Grace shows us that the transcendent is accessible in everything. This means that our birth was a grace and the events of our lives have been graces too, every one without exception. Death will also be a graced moment of letting go.

Grace is not elitist. It loves to make its way through our fragmentations, our mistakes, our shortcomings, our inclinations, no matter how dark. Grace can also shine through our talents, our healthy commitments, our good deeds, our heroic acts. Grace cuts through the dualism of what seems worse and what seems better in human choices. It is the opportunity in all of our choices.

As we have seen throughout the chapters of this book, everything that has ever happened to us has offered us a grace because all of it had the capacity to support our evolution toward greater psychological health and deeper spiritual progress. Since both psychological and spiritual growth are what make us more richly human, every opening into them is a path to manifesting our wholeness. The openings are so many graces; the wholeness is a grace.

Our psychological health involves attending to the central features of every human life: leftover issues from childhood, fulfillment of our needs, discovery of happiness, growth in self-esteem, liberty to show our feelings, the capacity to love ourselves and others, skill in establishing and maintaining effective loving bonds in social, work, familial, and intimate relationships.

Our spiritual life involves letting go of ego; loving unconditionally; growing in universal compassion; acting with wisdom; cocreating a world of justice, peace, and love; finding the wellsprings of joy in being human. To manifest all of this, we practice mindfulness and loving-kindness. Mindfulness makes us more human because we cease to be directed by ego, with its constricting judgments and compulsions. Loving-kindness makes us more humane, since it expands our ability to fulfill our central reason for being here: to love ourselves and everyone.

The fact that love is the goal of work and practice is what makes our joy so enduring. The nineteenth-century British prime minister William Gladstone wrote (according to *The Forbes Book of Business Quotations*): "We look forward to the time when the Power of Love will replace the Love of Power. Then will our world know the blessings of peace." The word *blessings* refers to the graces that come to everyone when love, our lushest grace, becomes all we do and are.

Now only grace abides, the tireless usher still escorting us—and every shimmering star—into the single, ceaseless Smile of all that is, or was, or shall be.

About the Author

David Richo, PhD, MFT, is a psychotherapist and workshop leader who lives in Santa Barbara and San Francisco, California. He combines Jungian, Buddhist, and mythic perspectives in his work. He is the author of the following books and audio from Shambhala Publications:

*Shadow Dance: Liberating the Power and
Creativity of Your Dark Side* (Shambhala Publications, 1999)

The shadow is all that we abhor about ourselves and also all the dazzling potential that we doubt or deny we have. We project these onto others as dislike or admiration. We can acknowledge our limitations and our gifts. Then both our light and dark sides become sources of creativity and awaken our untapped potential.

*How to Be an Adult in Relationships: The Five Keys
to Mindful Loving* (Shambhala Publications, 2002)

Love is not so much a feeling as a way of being present. Love is presence with these five A's: unconditional attention, acceptance, appreciation, affection, and allowing others to be as they are. Love is presence without the five conditioned overlays of ego: judgment, fear, control, attachment, and illusion.

*The Five Things We Cannot Change: And the Happiness We
Find by Embracing Them* (Shambhala Publications, 2005)

There are unavoidable "givens" in life and relationships. By our unconditional yes to these conditions of existence, we learn to open, accept, even embrace our predicaments without trying to control the outcomes. We begin to trust what happens as gifts of grace that help us grow in character, depth, and compassion.

The Power of Coincidence: How Life Shows Us What
We Need to Know (Shambhala Publications, 2007)

There are meaningful coincidences of events, dreams, or relationships that happen to us beyond our control. These synchronicities influence the course of our life in mysterious ways. They often reveal assisting forces that are pointing us to our unguessed, unexpected, and unimagined destiny.

Making Love Last: How to Sustain Intimacy and Nurture
Genuine Connection (set of 3 CDs, Shambhala Audio, 2008)

Here is a lively workshop given by David Richo at Spirit Rock retreat center in California on relationship issues. These are some of the topics: how love can endure, fears of intimacy and commitment, trust and fidelity, resolving our conflicts, the phases of a relationship, how our early life affects our adult relationships.

When the Past Is Present: Healing the Emotional Wounds That
Sabotage Our Relationships (Shambhala Publications, 2008)

Transference is a tendency to see our parents or other significant characters in our life story in others. We explore how our past impacts our present relationships. We find ways to make transference a valuable opportunity to learn about ourselves, deepen our relationships, and heal our ancient wounds.

Being True to Life: Poetic Paths to Personal Growth
(Shambhala Publications, 2009)

Poetry may have seemed daunting in school, but here is a chance for it to become quite wonderfully personal and spiritually enriching. This book offers an opportunity to use our hearts and pens to release the full range of our imagination and discover ourselves through reading and writing poetry.

Daring to Trust: Opening Ourselves to Real Love and Intimacy
(Shambhala Publications, 2010)

We learn how to build trust, how to recognize a trustworthy person, how to work with our fears around trusting, and how to rebuild trust after a breach or infidelity. We find ways to trust others, to trust ourselves, to trust reality, to trust what happens to us, and to trust a higher power than ourselves.

*Coming Home to Who You Are: Discovering Your Natural Capacity
for Love, Integrity, and Compassion* (Shambhala Publications, 2011)

Here are practices that can usher us into a new way of being alive—as
cheerful agents of the goodness that is in all of us. Our choices for integrity
and loving-kindness reflect that goodness and help us cocreate a world of
justice, peace, and love. This is an owner's guide to being an upright and
loving human.

*How to Be an Adult in Love: Letting Love in Safely and
Showing It Recklessly* (Shambhala Publications, 2013)

We explore ways to love ourselves without guilt and with generosity. We
learn how to love others with awareness of our boundaries. We confront our
fears of love and loving. We embrace the spiritual challenge of letting our
scope of love expand. Then love is a caring connection—unconditional,
universal, and joyous.

Embracing the Shadow: Discovering the Hidden Riches in Our Relationships
(set of 4 CDs, Shambhala Audio, 2013)

We work with our unskillful tendencies in our relationships so that we can
tame them and grow because of them. We notice our projections onto one
another. We find the gifts we might not yet have dared to recognize or show.
Working *with* the dark rather than *in* it lets the light of intimacy through.
This set of CDs is from a workshop given at Spirit Rock Buddhist retreat
center in California.

How to Be an Adult in Relationships
(read by the author; Shambhala Publications, 2013; audiobook)

For more information, including upcoming events and a catalog of audio/
video programs, visit davericho.com.